EX LIBRIS

A SUSSEX GUIDE

THE COUNTY OF SUSSEX

RYE

HASTINGS

EAST GRINSTEAD

A265

GATWICK

HAYWARDS HEATH

HEATHFIELD

DITCHLING

EASTBOURNE

A272

LEWES

A259

A23

BRIGHTON

A23

HORSHAM

A272

WORTHING

A27

MIDHURST

A272

CHICHESTER

ENGLISH CHANNEL

DITCHLING WALKS
IN ERIC GILL'S
FOOTSTEPS

LORRAINE HARRISON

FOREWORD BY
NATHANIEL HEPBURN

Maps by
SARAH YOUNG

SNAKE RIVER PRESS

SNAKE RIVER PRESS

Book No 21
Books about Sussex for the enthusiast

Published in 2017 by
SNAKE RIVER PRESS
South Downs Way, Alfriston, Sussex BN26 5XW
www.snakeriverpress.co.uk

ISBN 978-1-906022-20-4

This book was conceived, designed and produced by
SNAKE RIVER PRESS

ART DIRECTOR & PUBLISHER *Peter Bridgewater*
PAGE MAKEUP *Richard Constable*
ILLUSTRATOR *Sarah Young*
EDITOR *Jennifer Davis*

This book is typeset in Perpetua & Gill Sans,
two fonts designed by Eric Gill

Printed and bound in China

———

DEDICATION

For PGB with thanks

CONTENTS

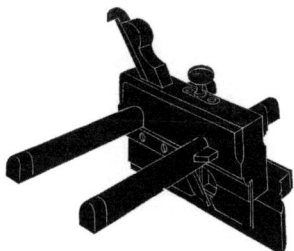

FOREWORD

There are many reasons to visit the small village of Ditchling. I hope that the museum is one, but it may also be the vineyards from where some of the best English sparkling wines are made, or the lively open houses trail taking place at various points in the year, or to stay in one of the campsites and of course to enjoy the hospitality in the fine pubs and tea rooms. Whatever your reason for visiting the village, the artistic heritage of Ditchling and the stunning landscape of the South Downs National Park would be hard to ignore.

Although Ditchling Museum of Art + Craft houses many of the works of art by the village's most famous residents, barely a step can be taken in the village without finding evidence of the artistic heritage: a discarded piece of carved lettering from Gill's workshop found and set into a wall, a church curtain hand-woven from the wool of Sussex sheep, a Brangwyn design plaque high on a cottage wall. The village is proud of its artistic heritage. Many of the plaques marking artists' homes have been commissioned from exceptional lettercutters, both celebrating and continuing the importance of this craft in the village Gill once called home. Walking the village streets, it can at times feel like every house was once occupied by an artist or craftsman.

Many of Ditchling's artistic community were members of the Guild of St Joseph and St Dominic and their work can be found in the churches and burial grounds of Ditchling and surrounding villages and towns. Artists who you would normally travel to a major city art gallery to experience can be found here in alleyways, in side chapels and in the long grass of a burial ground. Many businesses in the village make sure they use one of Eric Gill's typefaces and it is the only place I know where a villager will criticise the kerning on a shop sign.

One of the factors that drew many of Ditchling's artists was the exceptional landscape: the steep incline of Ditchling Beacon to the south, the South Downs stretching along the horizon and Lodge Hill rising on the north of the village, giving views over its picturesque rooftops. Since I arrived in Sussex the Snake River Press books have been my guide on many walks, teaching me the artistic landmarks, the best paths and the nicest pubs. It has been an honour to work together on this latest addition to their wonderful catalogue of books, which celebrate the landscape and artistic heritage of a county that I adore. I hope that through this book you will enjoy discovering more about the artists and craftspeople whose work is held in the Ditchling Museum of Art + Craft collection, and who made Ditchling famous across the world.

NATHANIEL HEPBURN

Director, Ditchling Museum of Art + Craft

INTRODUCTION:
WHY DITCHLING?

*'We thought that the place in England that had the greatest vitality
of thought and action in craftsmanship was probably the small village of
Ditchling ... just north of the Downs near the coast at Brighton.'*
BERNARD LEACH

During the first half of the 20th century several hitherto seemingly unremarkable places in England began to attract some very remarkable groups of creative people. This is especially true for the visual arts; one thinks of St Ives in Cornwall and Great Bardfield in Essex, for example. The small village of Ditchling in East Sussex was one such location and, as Ewan Clayton later noted, it was 'a place, a community of persons and a guiding dream'. This 'guiding dream' remained potent and alive for many decades and continued to thrive long after its most famous protagonist had upped sticks and left.

Craftsman Eric Gill came to Ditchling with his family and his assistant, Joseph Cribb, in 1907, a move that was to have a profound and far-reaching effect on the village. Ditchling literally nestles under the South Downs and the ridge of Ditchling Beacon, one of the highest points of the Downs, provides the distinctive horizon line to the south. This is land that has long been settled; there is an Iron Age fort here, while a Roman road and ancient droveways dissect the ground around the village. For centuries the main occupation of the inhabitants of Ditchling was agriculture, although in the 19th century there was a thriving trade in brick-making as locals began to exploit the heavy clay found at the base of the Downs. Hilary Pepler, with Esther Meynell, wrote *The Story of Ditchling* in 1946. As Pepler had known the village from soon after Gill's arrival, his view of the place is of particular interest:

*There is quite a different kind of life in Ditchling from that of its larger
neighbours, and it is largely conditioned by the cultivation of the land; that is
by the claims of agriculture in and by which the village has been moulded*

since the beginning of time. That life is a stable and continuous life; witness the names which appear on the rolls, tombstones, Parish Registers and Wills, for the last 600 hundred years ... for while the land remains to be cultivated and men cannot wholly subsist upon chemicals, those who work it tend to love rather than leave it.

In the early decades of the 20th century, as elsewhere in the country, the coming of the motor car changed forever the character of Ditchling, eventually turning it from a largely agricultural village to one that is today primarily residential, with easy access to Lewes, Brighton and even London. Anxiety about the changing face of Britain, especially the rural scene, was such that at the outbreak of WWII The Pilgrim Trust funded a project called Recording Britain. Almost 100 artists were commissioned to produce watercolours of places across the country. Ditchling was one of the first villages to be recorded, with many views painted by watercolourist and local resident Charles Knight.

Hilary Pepler's daughter Susan Falkner has written movingly about the lost idyll that was this corner of rural Sussex a century ago:

We were probably the last generation of children to enjoy the freedom of the glorious unpolluted countryside. The air and the waters were pure and the earth grew the most marvellous abundance of flowers. We knew the fields where the cowslips and early purple orchids grew. Earlier in the spring we would make expeditions to the wild daffodil places ... the woods then were literally carpeted with primroses. Wild columbine grew on the Common which, in March, would be white with wood anemones as if it had snowed. We knew where to find the bee orchids on the Downs and the woods where the butterfly orchids grew. Wandering home on a summer's evening there would be the little lights of glow worms at the roadside.

When reading this it is easy to understand what attracted not only Gill and his associates to Ditchling but also a long line of other artists. Along with Knight, the list of artists who have lived in Ditchling is a long one: the painters Frank Brangwyn and Louis Ginnett, the potter Bernard

Leach, the sculptor and inventor Rowland Emett, to name just a few. This tradition continues today with illustrators Raymond Briggs and John Vernon Lord, who both still live in the area.

The Guild of SS Joseph & Dominic

In 1920 Eric Gill, Hilary Pepler, Desmond Chute and Joseph Cribb founded the Guild of SS Joseph & Dominic (although their community of Roman Catholic craftsmen had already been in existence informally for some time). The original medieval guilds were associations of merchants and artisans that promoted high standards of workmanship and protected their members' interests. In the 19th century the Arts & Crafts Movement revived this model, creating modern-day guilds such as the Guild of St George and The Art Workers Guild. The ideas expressed in AJ Penty's *The Restoration of the Guild System* (1906) had a profound influence on Gill and his co-founders. Christianity was their founding principle, as opposed to the secular socialist ideals on which many of the Arts & Crafts communities, influenced by John Ruskin, William Morris and others, were based, although it is true to say that they shared the common ideals of anti-capitalism and anti-industriali-sation. Gill, Pepler, Chute and Cribb sought to integrate their religious beliefs and artistic endeavours into all aspects of everyday life; indeed, the Guild's constitution begins, 'That all work is ordained to God and should be Divine worship'.

Gill and Pepler collaborated with their friend Edward Johnston on a little magazine called *The Game*, which was in some ways a vehicle for working out many of their ideas as well as a great source of fun and entertainment. In an issue of 1921 Gill and Pepler wrote,

> Since the first number of The Game in 1916 we have been concerned in arriving at a way of life and work which would not be the denial of individualism but the affirmation of Truth. Last year we had arrived at a sufficiently clear agreement to make possible the beginning of a society or Guild. This Guild has taken SS Joseph and Dominic for its patrons.

St Joseph is the patron saint of workers, in particular of carpenters, and St Dominic of astronomers and scientists. A dog, one of the emblems of St Dominic, later became the symbol for Pepler's St Dominic's Press. It is shown carrying a torch, presumably to suggest light and illumination.

The other great influence on the founders of the Guild was Father Vincent McNabb (1868-1943), whom Gill and Pepler had met as early as 1917. A well-known Dominican theologian and social critic, it was under McNabb's influence that the two men became Dominican tertiaries (lay members of the order living in the community). McNabb believed in the social philosophy of distributism, one of the main tenets of which was the belief that the family, rather than the individual, was the basic unit of society. The writers Hilaire Belloc and GK Chesterton were also advocates of the system. McNabb also subscribed to the ideology of the back-to-the-land movement that was so current at the time. He believed that if Catholic families settled in the country their numbers would strengthen and he urged believers to 'Till your soil or kill your soul'. He favoured pre-industrial agricultural practices and self-sufficiency (the distributist slogan was 'Three acres and a cow'). For him, the medieval craft guild was the perfect model for the perfect life.

McNabb hoped that the Guild of SS Joseph & Dominic would be the first of many Catholic guilds to be established throughout the British Isles, setting a standard for others to follow. One of its aims states, 'The love of God means that work must be done according to an absolute standard of reasonableness; the love of our neighbour means that work must be done to an absolute standard of serviceableness. Good quality is therefore twofold, work must be good in itself and good for use.'

Long before the Guild was formed the Gills were already established on Ditchling Common, in a house called Hopkins Crank, where they had lived since 1913 (the family had previously lived at Sopers in Ditchling High Street). Gill had wished to put some distance between himself and the village and this feeling only increased as the Guild developed. A member of the Pepler family, Susan Falkner, has written,

I seem to remember the Common looked down upon the village from rather lofty heights – the attitude of the converted to the unconverted, I suppose. And this attitude seemed to be shared, however unconsciously, by that nucleus of men who made up the Guild, a holier-than-thou feeling, a sense of superiority.

Over the years a growing number of craftsmen, followers and idealists joined Gill on the Common, including Pepler and Chute. Gill and Pepler extended and added to existing buildings as demand increased for workshops and living space (in 1922 the community numbered 41 Catholics). By this time Pepler owned a farm beside the Common, worked by mainly pre-industrial methods. At the Guild, what had at first been makeshift buildings were gradually replaced by more substantial brick-built structures. The most important was the chapel; Susan Falkner has left an evocative first-hand account of her experience of worship there.

How vivid it is to me still – the feel of the place on a cold winter's morning as we sat in our damp clothes having traipsed over the fields in the rain. Then again, on a brilliant summer morning, our feet would be wet with the dew of the hay meadow. I remember the feel of kneeling on those flat leather hassocks on the rough brick floor and the scrape of wooden benches as we all took our seats again. The men who were tertiaries faced each other across the Chapel and the rest of us, the hoi polloi, faced the altar, of course – the design of a very primitive Priory church. It was a simple faith we had, nurtured by beauty and simplicity of the Chapel itself.

An important ethos of the Guild was the close integration of working and domestic life, something that remained important to Gill throughout his life. His aim was to produce beautiful objects for everyday use in what he referred to as 'common life', not highly priced luxury items for the wealthy. Skilled handiwork was seen as a kind of prayer or meditation. The Guild buildings bore a stone panel (made by Cribb and now in Cheltenham Museum) that read '*Homines divites in virtute pulchri-tudinis stadium habentes pacificantes in domibus suis* – Men rich in virtue, studying beautifulness: living at peace in their houses'.

Sadly, however, all was not peaceful. Personal and financial tensions developed between Gill and other Guild members, in particular with Hilary Pepler. There was also a relentless stream of visits from enthusiastic admirers or the simply curious. These pressures eventually resulted in Gill's decision to move to the more remote Welsh hills with his family to set up a new crafts community and he formally resigned from the Guild of SS Joseph & Dominic in July 1924. Looking back in 1950, Desmond Chute wrote, 'when life at Ditchling was spoilt by unwelcome publicity, he went to the wilds of Wales'. Many of the interpersonal scars left in the wake of his departure never truly healed. The Guild continued for well over 60 years; activities undertaken at various times included stone carving, woodworking, printing, book binding, weaving, engraving and silversmithing. Craftsmen worked independently both artistically and financially but would also collaborate on projects when appropriate.

By the early 1930s McNabb's influence was on the wane. Craftsmen (and mostly it was craftsmen as by and large women were never properly integrated into the workshop system) came and went while internal politics and financial difficulties ebbed and flowed over the years. One serious check on the development and growth of the Guild was the restrictions caused by the lack of accommodation, both domestic and commercial. Financial problems put a severe strain on the Guild in the 70s and 80s. Added to this was the major damage done by the 1987 hurricane to the buildings, which were already in a parlous state. The last member to join the Guild was the calligrapher Ewan Clayton in 1983. Only a few years passed by before the land and workshops were finally sold on 30 June 1989.

Perhaps Gill should be allowed the last words here concerning the legacy of the Guild. In his *Autobiography*, 1940, he wrote,

> ...the chief influence at this time was our daily life as brethren of our Guild. In the course of time we built a small chapel and a quadrangle of workshops, and we endeavoured to unite the life of work with the life of prayer. Looking back at those years I find it impossible to think that we were not successful.

Ditchling Museum of Art + Craft

There is no better place to start to appreciate the special nature of the village and its former inhabitants than the Ditchling Museum of Art + Craft. The present museum stands on the site of a Victorian National School. Funded by public subscription in the 1830s, it remained the village school until 1983. The buildings and surrounding area then came under threat as a developer planned to turn the land into a housing estate. Local sisters Hilary and Joanna Bourne (by then in their 70s) were instrumental in saving the site, raising awareness and funds, and even using their own money to fund the purchase of the school. The buildings were converted into a local museum and opened in 1985 by the actor Donald Sinden, who grew up in the village. The Bourne sisters were both deservedly awarded British Empire Medals for their services to the museum.

In the early days of the museum the collection was very eclectic indeed: agricultural implements and shepherds' smocks sat alongside items donated by the Guild of SS Joseph & Dominic, including the chapel bell and vestments. After the Guild was disbanded, a gallery dedicated to displaying their work was opened in 1993. Then, in 2006, the Trustees of the museum began to draw up radical future plans for the buildings and its collection. Following a tireless effort led by Jenny KilBride to raise sufficient funds to build a new museum, a Heritage Lottery Fund grant was awarded and matching funding obtained. The result is the stunning construction we see today.

The new museum opened in 2013. Designed by Adam Richards Architects, the scheme cleverly incorporates aspects of the hitherto rather random collection of buildings into a new and cohesive whole. The Grade II listed cart lodge (formerly part of Ditchling Court Farm), which had stood empty for decades, now forms the entrance, café and shop of the new museum. The main focus of the collection is the Guild, its associates and the wider circle of artists connected with the village. Much attention is paid to the materials and tools used by practitioners, thus very much showcasing the *art* and *craft* of those represented. This is not just reflected in the displays but also in the building itself.

Along with the Main Gallery the museum comprises a Print Gallery, Reading Room and Learning Centre. In the delightful garden grow plants that feature in the weaver Ethel Mairet's *Book of Vegetable Dyes*. A Stanhope printing press from St Dominic's Press provides a splendid focus in the Print Gallery, which the architects have described as being 'placed where an altar in a chapel might be, as a reminder of the Ditchling artists' religious preoccupations'. The collection is a rich mine of drawings, paintings, sculptures, textiles, books, ephemera and diverse objects associated with Ditchling and its artists. Some are majestic, while others are altogether more domestic in scale. The museum has many of the original signs that once hung outside the workshops and homes of the Ditchling artists. These include the carved sign for Mairet's house, Gospels, and for the Ditchling Handworkers' Guild.

A specially constructed Cabinet of Curiosities houses changing displays. Carved letters and signs, hand-crafted wooden buttons, jewellery, along with pictures by various artists, including David Jones, Charles Knight, Frank Brangwyn and Louis Ginnett, all make the museum the best possible place to begin to understand the artistic phenomenon that is Ditchling.

Notes on the Walks

This book features six circular walks in and around the village of Ditchling. Its aim is to show the very special connections forged between the area and the various artists and craftspeople who have lived and worked here over the last hundred years or so. For ease of orientation all the walks start at the museum, except for the walk to Ditchling Common, which begins at the car park of the Ditchling Common Country Park. Approximate times are given for the walks although these will vary depending on the pace of the walkers, how long is spent at each location, weather, conditions underfoot, and so forth.

Several of the places of interest featured in the book are the houses that were formerly occupied by the artists and craftspeople of Ditchling. These are now private residences, therefore please show due respect and be sensitive to the privacy of the present inhabitants.

AROUND THE VILLAGE

WALK I

'*…to make a cell of good living in the chaos of our world.*'

ERIC GILL

T his walk is not only a very good introduction to the scale and layout of Ditchling but also aptly illustrates just what a magnet the village has been over time for a diverse and interesting range of artists and craftspeople. Although Eric Gill and his circle are the names most readily associated with this corner of Sussex, this walk will show just how many other talented people have been attracted to set up home here. It also includes a small diversion to the Unitarian Chapel to see a grave carved by Joseph Cribb.

Villagers are rightly proud of their artistic heritage and many houses display plaques commemorating their former inhabitants. However, do be mindful that above all these are now private homes so please respect the privacy and space of the current residents as you enjoy this walk. The circular route should take around one and a half hours.

Crossways

From the museum turn left into West Street and continue until the road meets the junction with South Street and High Street. The 16th-century timber-framed house on the right hand corner is Crossways. This was home to the artist and calligrapher Lawrence Christie in the early 20th century. Like Gill, Christie was a pupil of Edward Johnston in Hammersmith, London. He and Gill formed a partnership as 'Inscriptional Carvers and Calligraphers', which was disbanded in 1908 after Gill had moved to Ditchling.

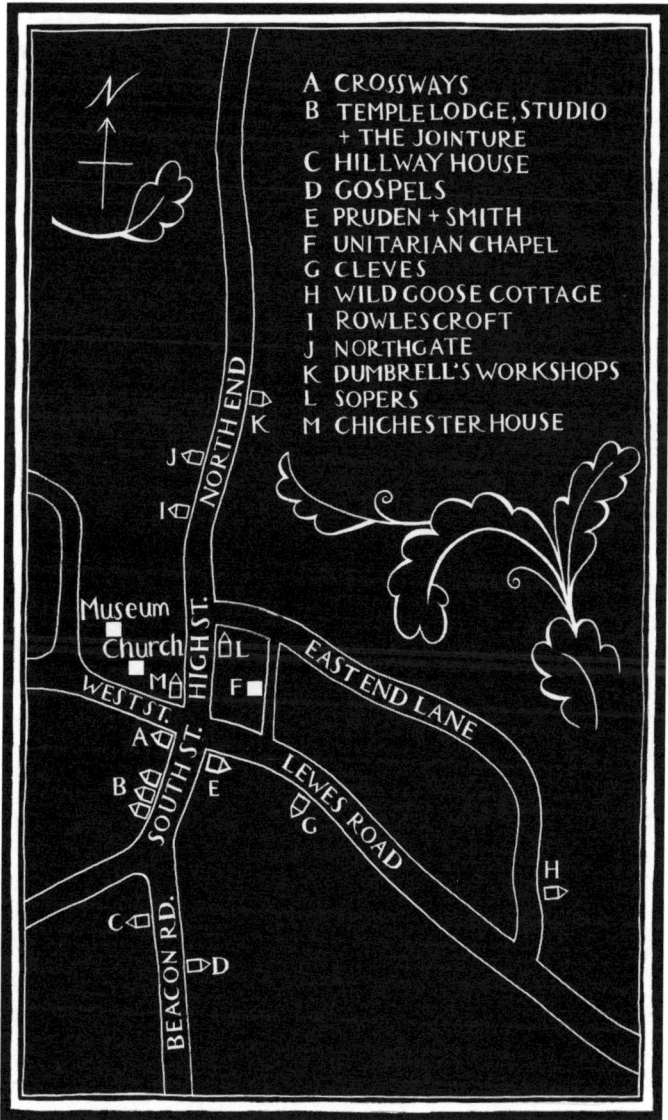

N

A CROSSWAYS
B TEMPLE LODGE, STUDIO + THE JOINTURE
C HILLWAY HOUSE
D GOSPELS
E PRUDEN + SMITH
F UNITARIAN CHAPEL
G CLEVES
H WILD GOOSE COTTAGE
I ROWLESCROFT
J NORTHGATE
K DUMBRELL'S WORKSHOPS
L SOPERS
M CHICHESTER HOUSE

NORTH END

K

J

I

Museum
Church
HIGH ST.
L
F
WEST ST.
M
EAST END LANE
A
SOUTH ST.
B
E
LEWES ROAD
G
BEACON RD.
C
H
D

NB. *This map is not to scale.*

Later, Crossways was home and surgery to the much-loved local physician Dr Linton-Bogle. Gill's nephew, John Skelton, carved the commemorative plaque, which reads: 'In grateful affection for the life of our Doctor Frederick Wallace Linton-Bogle who practised hereabouts and died in 1965 "*Guerir quelquefois, soulager souvent, consoler toujours*" [To heal sometimes, to relieve often, to comfort always].'

Temple Lodge, Studio & The Jointure

Continue a little way along South Street to number 9. It was while staying at a house called Coombe Down Lodge beneath Ditchling Beacon in 1917 that the artist Frank Brangwyn and his wife, Lucy, found and purchased this row of buildings in South Street. At that time what is now number 9 was at least two cottages and Brangwyn converted them to a single dwelling, naming it Temple Lodge after his former home in London. He gifted it to his faithful housekeeper Mrs Peacock in 1937. Number 13 became his studio and number 15 his home, The Jointure, from 1918 to 1956.

Brangwyn carried out extensive alterations to the property, commenting, 'I compulsively put brick on brick, throwing up an arch here and a buttress there.' Throughout the house the couple's initials L&FB, intertwined and set around a cross and a heart, were used as a motif in woodwork and plaster. Despite living in such a central position in the village Brangwyn was not often seen in the community. However, if in need of a model he would emerge from his studio and ask passers-by to pose for him! Some of these village models appear in the murals he painted for the Rockefeller Center in New York.

Internally the studio is two storeys high and note how the front door and window above are joined. This allowed them to be opened together so Brangwyn's very large canvases could be taken in and out of the studio with greater ease. Brangwyn had known Gill, Pepler and Johnston in Hammersmith but never became a member of the Guild of SS Joseph & Dominic. As an artist he was hugely successful and in the 1930s was known as 'Britain's most famous artist'. The 'Sussex Heritage Trust 2002' plaque to the right of the door was carved by Paul Wehrle, who was apprenticed to John Skelton. It denotes the granting of a Small Scale Residential Award for the conversion and renovation of the studio to a home and gallery at the turn of the century.

Behind the fine Georgian façade of The Jointure lies the original timber frame (it had been a medieval hall house and was rebuilt in the 17th century). Its name is a reference to the then unusual practice of joint tenancy of property between a husband and wife. A plaque bears the inscription 'Sir Frank Brangwyn R.A. 1867-1956 Painter, Etcher, lived, worked and died here'.

Following his wife's death in 1924, Brangwyn became increasingly pessimistic (although it is thought that they had not been that happily married). He certainly had health issues but was also given to bouts of hypochondria, although he did not in fact die until he was 89, in this house. He is buried at Kensal Green Cemetery in London.

Hillway House

Walk down South Street and turn into Beacon Road. A short way along on the right is Hillway House, an attractive red brick Arts & Crafts house. The Yorkshire architect Arthur Penty associated with members of the Guild and was in sympathy with their views on architectural form. He designed this house for himself and work began in 1924, only to be halted when he found out that the house opposite was a nursing home for sufferers of leprosy. (This is now number 20 and its name, Greyladies, is thought to allude to the grey attire of the nursing staff.) It was eventually completed in 1930 and is one of the few buildings in Ditchling built in the Arts & Crafts style.

Gospels

Cross over Beacon Road and walk a little way along until you reach Gospels, a brick detached house. From 1920 this was home to the weaver Ethel Mairet and her husband Philip, a writer, philosopher, ecologist and actor (they divorced in 1931). Hilary Pepler first invited the Mairets to visit him in Ditchling in 1916. They met Johnston, Gill and other craftsmen on this visit and were much attracted to the ethos of the community. When Philip was offered a job working on Pepler's farm in 1918, they decided to move. At first they lived at Sundown Cottage in Beacon Road. Later this became the home of Ethel's brother Fred Partridge and his second wife, Nellie. She and his other sister, Maud, ran it as the Sundown Tearooms and Fred, a silversmith and woodworker, set up a workroom on the first floor.

The Mairets purchased the land for Gospels in 1918 and Gill cut the date 'July 1919' into the foundation stone. He also designed the carved oak sign for Ethel's workshop when she moved into the house (this is now in the museum). Gill presented her with a wonderful carved garden roller; on one side is inscribed 'For the grass that has often times been trampled under foot give it time it will rise up again', while the other reads 'Come all you false young men do not leave me here to complain'. The Mairets commissioned the house to be built in an Arts & Crafts style but also wished to incorporate features from Ethel's former home in Gloucestershire, a converted Norman chapel restored by the Arts & Crafts architect CR Ashbee. Ernest Gimson supplied the oak exterior doors for Gospels.

Incorporated into the house was a weaving workshop and dye house. For 32 years Ethel trained people in the arts of hand-weaving and dyeing, producing simple cloth in plain weaves and strong vegetable-dyed colours. Known as 'The mother of English hand-weaving', Ethel was an influential teacher whose pupils included Valentine KilBride and Gill's daughter Petra. As well as training apprentices at Gospels, Ethel also employed local girls, usually four at a time, and their jobs included spinning, making warps and weaving. Hilary Bourne remembers that Ethel Mairet 'kept very much to herself, she didn't mix with the village nor did any of her workers'. However, she was an important figure in the creative life of the village although she never became a member of the Guild of SS Joseph & Dominic.

The potters Bernard Leach and Shoji Hamada were great admirers of Ethel Mairet's work. They first met her when visiting Frank Brangwyn. Hamada remembered having at meal at Gospels on a later visit: 'She served us dinner using a complete set of slipware ... The large and small pitchers, oval dishes and green plates all went well with the large oak table.' Ethel grew dye plants in her garden and would also collect weld while walking up on the Downs. Initially she wove with wool – her favourite fleece was that of the Southdown breed of sheep – although later she also used cotton and silk. CR Ashbee described Gospels and Ditchling in the early 1920s with 'Ethel in the centre of it all with her wonderful weaving workshops, her looms and carpets and dyed stuffs. She has the soul of Oriental colour in her.'

Pruden & Smith

Retrace your steps back along Beacon Road and South Street to the shop on the corner of South Street and Lewes Road, opposite Crossways. What is now Pruden and Smith's silversmith shop stands on the site of what was the old workhouse, demolished in 1873. The windows date from when it was a butcher's shop. In the 1930s it became the offices of the Ditchling Press (formerly St Dominic's Press). Hilary Pepler moved the press from Ditchling Common after he left the Guild and the print workshops ran along the east side of South Street until the 1980s. The press then moved to Burgess Hill, the buildings were demolished and the new houses you see now were erected on the site. Goldsmith and silversmith Dunstan Pruden became a member of the Guild in 1934 and his grandson Anton continues the family tradition working from these premises with Rebecca Smith, offering free tours of their workshop.

Unitarian Chapel

Cross over Lewes Road and a little way along you will find a twitten (the Sussex term for a narrow path or alleyway). Follow the twitten until you come to the pretty Unitarian Chapel on the left (signposted as the Old Meeting House). Just left of the building by the gateway to the Garden of Remembrance is a gravestone carved by Gill's former assistant, Joseph Cribb. It is the third stone along and reads 'In loving memory of Hilda Caroline Adney born 13th Jan 1881 died 12th May 1932'. Retrace your footsteps back to Lewes Road.

Cleves

Turn left, and continue along the Lewes Road until you come to the house known as Cleves (number 40). This was the home and workplace of Edward Johnston and bears a plaque with the simple inscription '1920 Edward Johnston Calligrapher Worked here and lived here 1944'. Johnston originally moved to Ditchling in 1912, prompted partially by the ill health of his wife, Greta, who had been diagnosed with tuberculosis, and also to work with Gill whom he had taught at the Central School of Arts & Crafts in London. In his *Autobiography* Gill wrote of the effect that seeing Johnston at work on his calligraphy had on him: 'I was struck by lightning, as by a sort of enlightenment. It was no mere dexterity that transported me; it was as though a secret of heaven were being revealed.'

At one point the Johnston and Gill families discussed building a house together that would be sheltered under the Downs. Their favoured design was a house set around a quadrangle that was entered through an archway. Johnston would have a scriptorium and Gill a workshop, but it was not to be. Johnston at first lived in the house next door to Cleves, called Downsview, then for a time at Hallets Farm on the Common near the Gills, but returned to the village in 1920 and settled at Cleves. Here he grew vegetables in the garden and kept chickens. It is said Johnston devised an ingenious system of pulleys that enabled him to open the chicken coop door in the morning without even leaving his bedroom! Although a devout man, neither he nor his wife, Greta, shared Gill's passionate enthusiasm for Roman Catholicism. He remained a hugely influential and guiding figure for many of the Ditchling artists but never became a Guild member. After the death of Greta in 1936 Johnston became increasingly reclusive and died here at home on 26 November 1944.

Wild Goose Cottage

Continue along Lewes Road then turn left into East End Lane. Pass the entrance to Emett Gardens on the right and Wild Goose Cottage is the detached cottage facing you. Until 1990 this was the home of the sculptor and inventor Rowland Emett. In 1951 he designed an installation called Emettiana for London's Battersea Park as part of the Festival of Britain celebrations. Emettiana's Far Tottering and Oystercreek Railway featured three flying engines, one of which was named Wild Goose. However, Emett's greatest claim to fame is the design of the car Chitty Chitty Bang Bang, star of the eponymous British film. *Time* magazine dubbed him a 'Fantasticator', proclaiming, 'No other term could remotely convey the diverse genius of the perky, pink-cheeked Englishman whose pixilations, in cartoon, watercolour and clanking 3-D reality, range from the celebrated Far Tottering and Oystercreek Railway to the demented thingamabobs that made the 1968 movie *Chitty, Chitty, Bang, Bang* a miniscule classic.' A man of great energy and application, Emett worked long days at his studio in Wild Goose Cottage while many of his large-scale creations were produced in a studio at the nearby village of Streat.

Rowlescroft

Walk to the top of East End Lane and turn right into North End. Along on the left side of the road is the lovely Georgian frontage of Rowlescroft, built c.1800. Like Crossways, this too was at one time home to the artist and calligrapher Lawrence Christie, co-founder of the Society of Scribes and Illuminators.

Northgate

Further along North End on the same side of the road is Northgate. The name of this pretty house refers to the siting of the toll house for the old turnpike road. This was home to the sisters Joanna and Hilary Bourne, the founders of the Ditchling Museum.

Dumbrell's Workshops

A little further along on the right are the Turner-Dumbrell Foundation's Workshops. The Dumbrell family were tenant farmers in the village in the 19th century and also established a school here at North End House. Much extended, this then became North End House School, later known as Dumbrells. Pupils included the Bourne sisters and HRH The Duchess of Cornwall. The Foundation was established in 1983 by a Dumbrell antecedent, Dr Richard Wainwright Duke Turner, then, following the sale of some of the land, the remaining dairy and five barns were converted into workshops. A range of local artists and craftspeople now work here and visitors are encouraged to visit the workshops and view their work. The silversmiths Pruden and Smith worked here before moving to their premises on the High Street and it is also home to the Edward Johnston Foundation.

Sopers

Stay on the same side of the road and head back towards the village centre. Just past the turning into East End Lane on the High Street is Sopers, which at different times was home to both the Gill and Pepler families. In the mid 17th century it was two houses; ghosts of the original front doors are still visible in the brickwork. Around 1790 it was turned into a single dwelling and assumed the more balanced Georgian façade we see today, with a neat porch and canopy. The upper part of the south wall has mathematical tiles. These glazed tiles were substituted for bricks to avoid the late 18th- and early 19th-century brick taxes.

In August 1907 Gill, with his wife Ethel, (later known as Mary after their conversion to Catholicism in 1913), and young daughters Betty and Petra, moved here from Hammersmith, having become increasingly disenchanted with city living. In many ways Sopers perfectly conformed to his early ideal of a 'four square building'. What is now the garage behind the house was used as his workshop and thus began the close integration of domestic life and working life that was to continue until Gill's death –what he later described as 'the idea that life and work and love and the bringing up of a family and clothes and social virtues and food and houses and games and songs and books should all be in the soup together'.

It was here in 1910 that the sculptor Jacob Epstein and Gill collaborated on several sculptures. Sadly their scheme for a series of huge sculpted human figures to sit in the Sussex landscape was never realised, even though a suitable site was found in the grounds of Asheham House, a few miles south-east of Lewes. (Now demolished, Asheham was briefly the first Sussex home of Virginia and Leonard Woolf.) They soon fell out but Gill still designed the inscriptions for Epstein's tomb of Oscar Wilde (located in the Père Lachaise Cemetery, Paris). Gill's apprentice, Joseph Cribb, went to Paris with Epstein to cut the inscription in 1912.

The kitchen at Sopers was large and became the symbolic centre of family life. It was here that the consumption of their nourishing home-made bread first assumed a near spiritual significance: the timeless ritual of breaking bread with family and friends. (Although several visitors later recounted less enthusiastically that they found the Gills' bread as heavy and unpalatable as it was wholesome!) The Gills' Sussex home soon became a magnet for visitors both famous and obscure; Leonard and Virginia Woolf and the poet Rupert Brooke were among the many who sat around the scrubbed kitchen table at Sopers. The Gill's third child, Joan, was born in this house in 1910. The plaque to the left of the front door was carved by Jack Trowbridge, one of Skelton's apprentices, and states simply 'Eric Gill Sculptor Lived Here 1907-1913'.

The Gills moved northwards to Ditchling Common in 1913. Hilary Pepler took over Sopers in 1915, having written to Johnston 'Can you think of any work I can do in Ditchling? We want an excuse to follow the prophet (you) into the wilderness.' Soon after, he installed a Stanhope hand printing press in the workshop. He had brought it from London to Sussex, along with two founts of Caslon Old Face and reams of Batchelor's handmade paper and set up St Dominic's Press at Sopers. In the following year he moved it to a specially designed printshop on the Common. (The press is now housed in the museum.) Alongside the high-minded texts printed by the press were some rather more prosaic productions, such as bottle labels for the Sandrock pub. (The original sign for The Sandrock Inn is still visible on the building to the right, now converted to flats.) In 1918, to celebrate the second anniversary of the founding of St Dominic's Press, Pepler penned the rhyme overleaf.

We printed large and black and clearly,
Way Ho, a-printing we will go.
We printed quite as well – or nearly
As the old printers printed printing long ago.
The sculptor did the very best he could
Way Ho, a-graving we will go.
To grave us pretty pictures upon the wood
As gravers graved graving long ago.

In the same year, Pepler and his family followed the Gills and moved up to the Common.

Chichester House

Cross over the road and carry on towards the bottom of the High Street. The large double-fronted Georgian building is Chichester House, the home of artist Louis Ginnett, whose studio was behind the house. Ginnett saw active service in WWI and trench scenes became one of his subjects. After the war he taught at the Brighton School of Art, where Charles Knight was one of his pupils. Neither Ginnett nor Knight became members of the Guild. Before Ginnett bought the house it had been the venue for the Chichester Working Men's Club, whose activities included cards, billiards and music. It had also been a library and coffee house until 1900.

Now turn right into West Street and then right again and you are back at the museum.

IN ERIC GILL'S FOOTSTEPS

TO DITCHLING COMMON & ST GEORGE'S RETREAT

WALK 2

'What I hope above all things is that I have done something towards re-integrating bed and board, the small farm and the workshop, the home and school, earth and heaven.'

ERIC GILL

D itchling Common and its surroundings are now very much changed from the days when the members of the Guild of SS Joseph & Dominic and their associates lived and worked there. Lying two miles to the north of Ditchling village, the area of the Common that was once occupied by the homes and workshops of the Guild is now an island of land pressed hard against the sprawling extremities of Burgess Hill. Save for a few houses, all that remain are ghosts and memories. Yet I advise you to stand on the site of the now lost buildings and gaze south towards the ridge of the Downs, ignore the noise of the traffic and imagine what it was like a century ago. How remote and morally bracing this place must have seemed, how conducive to simple living, to honest craft and creativity, and above all to a very particular type of muscular Christianity.

Although there is less to see here than in the village, the effort to visit the Common is well worth it, if you wish to gain an understanding of why Gill was drawn to move here with his young family in 1913. A visit to the Common serves to show the very real separation he was wishing to effect between the Gill family and the more conventional life of an English village. He later explained his position in a pamphlet he wrote for the Guild: 'In 1913 a Catholic family bought a house and two acres of land at the south end of Ditchling Common, one mile from St George's Retreat. Their object was to own home and land and to produce for their own consumption such food as could be produced at home, e.g. milk, butter, pigs, poultry and eggs, and to make such things as could be made at home, e.g. bread, clothes etc.'

If travelling by car, the most convenient place to start the walk is the car park of Ditchling Common Country Park, where there is ample parking. To complete the round trip from the car park to the site of the Guild houses and workshops and on to St George's Retreat and back again will take around two and a half hours. A little energy and a lot of imagination is needed to get the most out of this walk, and in wet weather a pair of wellingtons is also an essential as it can be very muddy underfoot! Several stiles will also need to be climbed. Not all the walk follows pavements and footpaths so please take extra care when walking alongside those areas of the B2112 and the road from the car park where there is no pavement. Be aware that the few houses associated with the Guild that are still extant are private dwellings: do please respect the privacy of the inhabitants and only view the exteriors from a comfortable distance. Likewise, St George's Park is now a care home and residential apartments so ensure you visit only the graveyard and no other areas of the park.

This walk falls naturally into two parts. The first walk takes you west from the car park to explore the houses associated with members of the Guild and the land where their workshops stood. The second part of the walk brings you back to the Country Park where you head north across Ditchling Common to visit the graveyard of St George's Retreat and back again. The graveyard is on private property so please ensure you contact St George's Retreat beforehand so that ground staff are aware of your presence. Call 01444 259725 ahead of your visit. Do please observe this courtesy, otherwise future access may be withdrawn.

Ditchling Common Country Park

Head out of Ditchling village northwards on the B2112 for about two miles until you come to a roundabout. Turn right here: a little way along on the left is the turning for the Country Park car park.

Hopkins Crank & Associated Houses

Leave the car park at the lower footpath entrance and turn right along the side of the road. Almost immediately, cross the road opposite the stile, which is marked by a yellow footpath sign. Climb over the stile and walk across the Common towards the railway straight ahead of you. This area of the Common is little changed from how it looked a century ago. On reaching the railway, turn right and follow the path towards the railway bridge. Cross the stile and walk around the crash barrier onto the road (B2112). Turn left and walk over the bridge and follow the road south a few metres until you are opposite a fine Georgian-fronted house. This is Hopkins Crank, home to the Gills. Cross the road and walk up the drive that passes in front of the house. From here you can see the plaque bearing Eric Gill's name. Much like Sopers in the village, this house conforms to his ideal of a 'four square house'. Desmond Chute described it as 'a neat square toy of a house on the western fringe of the Common, an untouched Georgian squatter's cottage, preceded by a porch and diminutive fenced garden'.

The money to buy Hopkins Crank was borrowed from Mary's uncle and Gill saw the move as a realisation of his desire to live 'a normal life', which for him was the life little changed from that of a medieval labourer. When the Gills arrived here in 1913 they had three daughters, Betty aged 8, Petra aged 7 and Joan aged only 3, and all were home educated. Gill also longed for a son and while living at Hopkins Crank they adopted a boy called Gordian, although the arrangement was never formalised.

Mary dealt with all the family's domestic chores, which were not insubstantial. Above and beyond the demands of house and family there was the keeping of chickens, pigs and a cow. Gill considered it a 'law of nature' that the domestic sphere 'must naturally be the woman's domain'. In his *Autobiography*, 1940, he contrasted 'the tired business-woman' with her accompanying 'tinned foods in the cupboard and tailor-made clothes and golf' with 'the contented housewife and mother

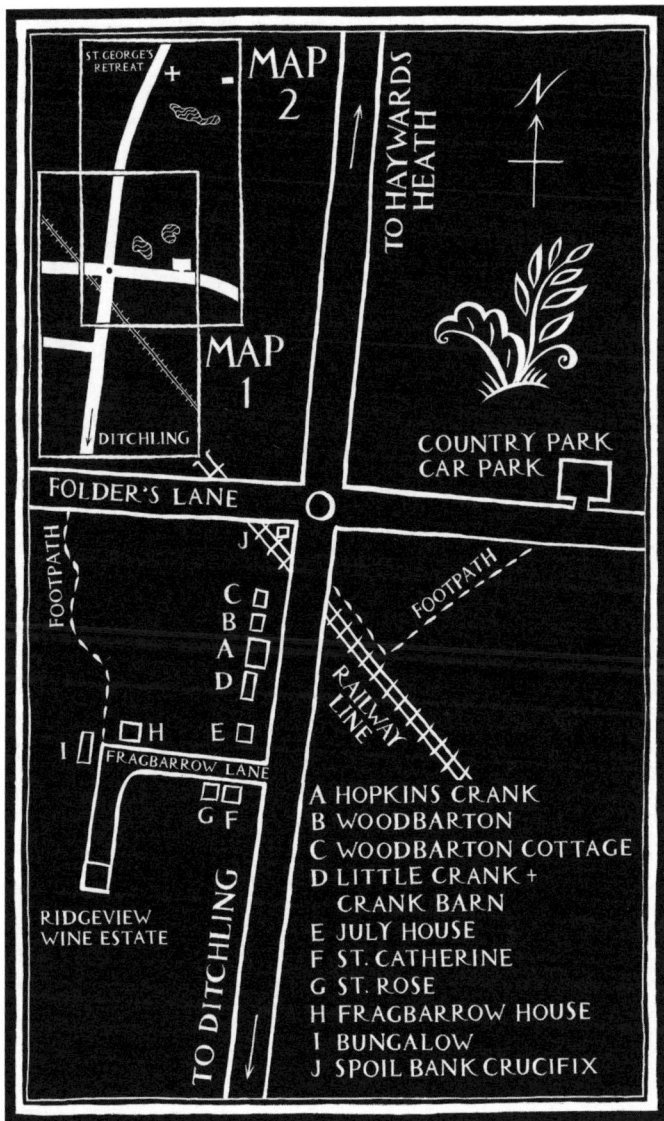

ST.GEORGE'S RETREAT

MAP 2

TO HAYWARDS HEATH

N

MAP 1

DITCHLING

COUNTRY PARK CAR PARK

FOLDER'S LANE

FOOTPATH

FOOTPATH

J

C
B
A
D

E

RAILWAY LINE

H
I
FRAGBARROW LANE

G F

RIDGEVIEW WINE ESTATE

TO DITCHLING

A HOPKINS CRANK
B WOODBARTON
C WOODBARTON COTTAGE
D LITTLE CRANK +
  CRANK BARN
E JULY HOUSE
F ST. CATHERINE
G ST. ROSE
H FRAGBARROW HOUSE
I BUNGALOW
J SPOIL BANK CRUCIFIX

NB. *This map is not to scale.*

of children – mother, bed-companion, helpmate and comforter, cook, housewife, baker and wine-maker, seamstress and broideress; and very likely farm manager and poultry and dairy-woman as well'. It now seems miraculous that the long-suffering Mary fulfilled all these roles in the Gill family, often while at the same time her husband was entertaining one of his numerous mistresses.

Monastic historian Peter Anson recollected his experience of life on the Common in 1920: 'There was a certain Spartan simplicity about the domestic arrangements and a complete lack of what are known as "modern conveniences". Water was drawn from a pump. The lavatory was a two-seater earth closet housed in a little ivy-clad house in the orchard. Meals, though the food was abundant, were somewhat erratic, because all cooking was done on an open fire which burned logs.' Susan Falkner, Hilary Pepler's daughter, lived at Hopkins Crank in the 1920s and recalls 'trying to cook on the open fire in that great cold living-room. The fire always smoked unless you opened a window, which of course made the room colder still.'

As his biographer, Fiona MacCarthy, has noted, it appears Gill wished to exert control over all aspects of his working and domestic life and at times this manifested itself in startling ways, not least within his most intimate family relationships (many of which were often inappropriate). The British Museum's collection of Gill's work contains 148 drawings depicting sexual anatomy and acts of intimacy. These are primarily studies made from life, with his family, friends and assistants serving as models. In *Sculpture and the Living Model*, 1932, Gill wrote, 'The members of your own household and your friends and relations are the best models … it is among the things you love that you must choose the things to carve – or to draw, or to paint.'

Gill's need to state his case, to stand his ground, even extended to his mode of attire, which he somehow managed to integrate into his wider philosophy. On the Common he was mostly seen dressed in the smock of a medieval stonemason or on occasions a religious habit. He argued that his chosen clothing was 'rational' and suited to his working life, and his clothes were very much homewoven, homespun and homemade.

Gill owned smocks in both winter and summer weight fabrics: sometimes he wore drawers underneath, other times not (bear in mind that conditions on the Common in winter were spartan, monastic and very cold). It is reported that for formal occasions his underpants were made of red Ceylonese silk. In *Clothing Without Cloth*, 1931, he argued that 'clothes are primarily for dignity and adornment' and one feels that nakedness would probably have been his preferred state, for himself, and for his family and friends, had the Sussex climate been more clement. As so often happened, Gill caused something of a public stir when working on scaffolding outside Broadcasting House in London's Portland Place. While carving his sculpture *Prospero* and *Ariel* for the BBC, those passing below would often glance above to try to see what exactly he did, or did not, wear beneath his smock! Gill wrote several books on the psychology of dress and in later life he wore 'the girdle of chastity', a symbolic cord worn by the Confraternity of the Angelic Warfare, a branch of the Dominican Order.

Such was his charisma that where Eric Gill went, others followed and the community grew quickly. Hilary Pepler with his wife, Clare, moved to the Common a few years after Gill and Hopkins Crank became their family home in 1924, following Gill's move to Wales (just as he had moved into Gill's old house, Sopers, in the village). Their daughter Susan remembers Hopkins Crank at this time: 'The house, as left by the Gills, would have felt quite familiar to a family from medieval times. There had been absolutely no concessions made to domestic convenience – rather the contrary, it seemed.' Despite a certain upgrading of the living conditions at Hopkins Crank by the Peplers, when Father Brocard Sewell stayed there in the 30s things were still on the spartan side. He wrote, 'in winter the bedrooms were icy; to warm one's bed one took with one, (wrapped in a newspaper), a brick heated at the fire in the sitting room. All water was pumped by hand.' Of the chilly dining room Sewell remembered, 'In the middle of this lofty raftered room was a large dining table. In the winter, the household, with any visitors who might be present, sat round this table at meals wearing a full complement of hats, scarves and greatcoats.'

Pepler continued to live here even after he was asked to leave the Guild in 1936, following disagreements with fellow members over his employment of a non-Catholic apprentice, along with the introduction of more mechanised processes at St Dominic's Press. Pepler's partner, Cyril Costick, introduced to the press a treadle-operated machine that was later motorised. This was considered by other members to be very much against the ethos and spirit of the Guild. In a fit of pique, Pepler lit a big bonfire on the Common and set about burning items associated with the press. Fortunately a number of valuable items, including prints by David Jones, were rescued from the ashes. Pepler died at Hopkins Crank on 20 September 1951, having suffered a heart attack while working in the garden.

Woodbarton

Now follow the drive up to the right of Hopkins Crank to reach Woodbarton. Funded by Desmond Chute, it was designed by Gill and built in 1921. Inside are carvings by both Gill and Chute, along with fixtures from the woodworking workshop of George Maxwell. Chute lived here briefly, followed by Charlie Waters and his family. Waters was treasurer to the Guild and married to Gill's sister. Valentine and Cecilia KilBride moved into Woodbarton in 1929 and the family remained there until 1982. Edgar Holloway took up residence the following year, adding a studio and installing indoor plumbing in the house.

Woodbarton Cottage

At the end of the lane, hidden from view around the corner is Woodbarton Cottage. It was named by the three Gill daughters as The Sorrowful Mysteries, a wry comment on the young apprentices who lived there in the 1920s. It was here that David Jones lived when he came to the Common to find solace from the traumas he had suffered at the front during the war. Formerly the stable and carriage shed for Woodbarton, the building was cold and damp. Philip Hagreen remembered Jones at this period:

My main memory of David at Ditchling is of his utter goodness.
He had an awful lot to put up with and he never blamed anyone or
complained; the discomfort amounted almost to torment. He was lodged
in a stable … Around and under it lay the dregs of Noah's flood not
yet drained off. David's mattress grew mildew and I don't know why
he did not get rheumatic fever. Our workshop was a hut without
lining or ceiling. The wind blew between the weatherboards and the
floorboards. David pulled his belt tight to make his clothes hug him
and kept on working. At that time he produced an astonishing quantity
of engravings, drawings and carvings.

Despite these privations Jones later wrote, 'What a wonderful phase of one's life that Ditchling period was. When I think what I owe directly to Eric and then add what I owe indirectly to him it amounts to an enormous debt.' He learnt carving and wood engraving from Gill and also worked as an assistant to George Maxwell. Jones made many of the door handles for the buildings on the Common. Although it was said by some that Jones was a rather clumsy and inept carpenter, he became an expert carver of wood, making beautiful small statues and engraving blocks.

Jones became engaged to Gill's middle daughter, Petra, in 1924 (an arrangement she ended in 1927). To commemorate their engagement he produced the oil painting *The Garden Enclosed* (now in the collection of the Tate). It is named after the Old Testament Song of Songs iv:12, 'A garden enclosed is my sister, my spouse, a spring shut up, a fountain sealed'. As a romantic gesture it is a somewhat strange painting. It depicts two lovers set amid a bucolic idyll, the garden of Hopkins Crank, yet the girl appears to be pulling back from the proffered kiss of her lover. The figures are placed uncomfortably on the extreme right of the picture's frame while centre stage lies a discarded doll. Whatever might have been the pain associated with Petra the influence of her father on Jones remained undiminished throughout his life. In the early 1950s he wrote of Gill to a friend, 'I still think of him as a kind of Socrates'.

Little Crank & July House

Return down the drive to Hopkins Crank, where you will see a courtyard to the left of the house. These buildings, which were once the dairy and workshop, have now been converted into two houses, Little Crank and Crank Barn. Follow the road south a little way towards the Downs and you will pass July House. This was formerly known as Maryfield and was designed and built by Hilary Pepler in 1939 for his daughter Susan. The land on which it stands was called Mary's Field, named after Mary Gill.

St Catherine & St Rose

Just past July House turn right into Fragbarrow Lane (note the sign for Ridgeview Wine Estate). As you walk up the lane the first two houses on the left were designed by Gill and built by George Maxwell. The first house, St Catherine (now called Brambleside), was Philip Hagreen's home and later lived in by David Pepler and his wife, Betty (Gill's daughter). Pepler's sister Susan remembers it as a particularly cold house (even by the chilly standards of the Common's dwellings) as it even had brick floors upstairs. David and his family later moved to Billingshurst to farm where, tragically, he died of tuberculosis aged 29. Dunstan Pruden later lived briefly at St Catherine. From 1924 until 1959 Joseph Cribb and his wife Agnes lived next door at St Rose with their five children.

Fragbarrow House

At the top of the lane on the right is Fragbarrow House. This large Victorian building was home to the Peplers between 1919 and 1924 and was the farmhouse to Fragbarrow Farm. The building replaced an old Tudor house that had been bought by Americans and shipped for reconstruction in the States. If you follow the road round to the left you will come to Ridgeview Wine Estate, open to the public for tastings and sales (see *www.ridgeview.co.uk* for opening times). Take the footpath to the right of the bungalow in front of you. Cross over the stile and follow the footpath along the edge of the field until you reach a squeeze gate on your right. Go through the gate and continue to follow the footpath on your left, crossing another stile, until you reach Folders Lane. Cross the road and turn right towards the railway bridge. All the land to your right as far as the railway line was the area once occupied by the chapel, workshops, allotments and orchards of the Guild of SS Joseph & Dominic. The entrance to the workshops was originally opposite the last house on the left before the bridge. After the Guild closed in 1989 the land was sold to a developer and two houses were built where the workshops and chapel stood.

The Guild on Ditchling Common

It is hard to imagine today but this was once the site of a bustling community of Catholic craftsmen including sculptors, wood and stone carvers, dyers and weavers, silversmiths and printers. In 1919 the first workshops and houses had been constructed from surplus army huts, some of which were later replaced by more permanent structures. The brick-built workshops were intended to form a quadrangle with the chapel to the south but it was never completed. There was also a school-room for educating the children of Guild members. Originally Claire Pepler had run a small school for the younger children, aided by a series of governesses. She favoured the progressive Montessori method of education. Later, a designated school hut was built as part of the Guild complex and young Catholic girls were employed as teachers.

Central to the community was the chapel, built to Gill's design. Desmond Chute described the daily round of worship on the Common in a letter: 'We have an almost monastic life – Angelus rung – sung Compline followed by Rosary every night around a little Madonna of his [Gill's] making. The whole day is a round of praise, be it work or prayer; do you see my lives are fallen in a very pleasant and fruitful place, thank God.' Although somewhat reduced over time, daily prayer remained a constant throughout the life of the Guild and several of those living on the Common became Dominican tertiaries (lay members of the Dominican Order). In the chapel David Jones decorated the metal door of the sacristy safe, depicting the Lamb of God. Stone capitals were carved by Joseph Cribb for the chapel and two low relief stone carvings were placed either side of the altar: a Madonna and Child by Desmond Chute and St Joseph the Carpenter by Cribb. A crucifix by Gill hung above the chancel steps. The wooden benches were made in the Maxwell workshop while Valentine KilBride's workshop provided the vestments. A rug that lay in front of the altar was commissioned from Ethel Mairet.

An attempt was made to combine the art and craft work done by the community with the rigorous activity of agricultural labour. When Hilary Pepler arrived on the Common in 1917 he first lived on a small farm called Hallets but later bought the larger farm at Fragbarrow. This he and his eldest son, David, ran on pre-industrial principles: hay was cut with a scythe and corn with a swophook (as propounded by McNabb). Initially the premises had running water but no electricity. The integration of the farm with the artistic life of the Guild was very much part of the distributist philosophy that was so close to the hearts of Guild members. They were recruited to help on the farm at busy times in support of the belief that the community and its individual members should be self-supporting as far as possible. In reality the Guild of SS Joseph & Dominic was never self-sufficient, although Fragbarrow Farm certainly went some way to providing food for its members. In later years the farm passed into other hands and self-sufficiency became less important in the minds of Guild members.

As well as being an enthusiastic farmer and printer, Pepler was a keen puppeteer and converted one of his barns into a puppet theatre. There are several exhibits relating to this activity in the museum. It is probable that the theatricality of Catholic ritual and liturgy appealed to Pepler's sense of drama. One of his daughters recalled that 'he regarded the sanctuary as a stage and the rites of the Mass as a formalised dance'. St Dominic's Press published several of his plays for puppet theatres.

Although Eric Gill had undoubtedly provided the initial impetus for the creation of a community of Catholic craftsmen on Ditchling Common, following his departure in 1924 the strength and longevity of the community should in no way be underestimated. The spirit and ethos remained very much alive, as Jenny KilBride notes: 'Our houses were full of beautiful things made by Guild members and by using them every day we absorbed them completely into our lives and had no sense that they were "art" objects.' Through troughs and peaks the Guild continued, evolving and changing as the times demanded, until in 1989 the land and workshops were finally sold.

Spoil Bank Crucifix

After crossing over the railway bridge you can see the Common ahead of you once again. On your right is a small hill, now dense scrubland. This is where, before the trees grew up, Gill placed his great wooden calvary in full and revelatory view of the railway passengers speeding by. All that remains today is the brick base at the stop of the slope. A funding appeal was launched in 1919 to commission a crucifix to commemorate the dead of WWI. Measuring 26 feet tall, the wooden sculpture was erected in November 1922 on the brick plinth. It was removed in 1940, when it was feared that it could act as a landmark for enemy bombers, and relocated to the Guild workshops. The cross itself and the arms of the figure were lost during the war but what remained of the work was sold to Rensselaer Newman Foundation and is on display in their Chapel and Cultural Center in Troy, New York State. This area is designated as part of Ditchling Common and is open access land. Though the footpath is overgrown and impenetrable, making the base difficult to locate, it is worth the hunt to appreciate the scale of the missing cross.

When you reach the roundabout, cross over the B2112 opposite the Ditchling Road sign. Follow the pavement round to the right and, where it ends, take the footpath to your left. Follow this footpath until you reach the pond. This was a favourite spot where Guild children played, fished, picnicked and skated when the pond froze in cold winters. Walk along the edge of the pond and the footpath will lead you back to the car park.

St George's Retreat

If you wish to carry on to this second section of the walk, take the path that leads uphill on the right hand side of the cleared area above the pond. At the top, where the path curves round to the left, you will find a metal gate leading into the wooded area. The gate is sometimes hidden by bracken in summer. Go through the gate and turn left along the path. In a very short distance take the path to your right and follow it through the trees. In front of you there is a post with both a yellow and a blue arrow way marker. Take the direction of the yellow arrow. Follow the footpath, which takes you through high hedges. In summer this footpath can become quite overgrown with bracken and nettles so shorts and tee shirts are not advisable. About halfway along you will see the ponds: these were once the claypits for the brickworks that were on the Common, and are now duck ponds. At the end of the path turn sharp left through the gate. The path now leads downhill between two fences and with further stiles to cross until it crosses a farm track with farm buildings on either side. Cross the track and walk down the cart track straight ahead to the bottom of the hill. Here you will see a large pond to your left. Cross the bridge and go over a stile into the field ahead. The footpath follows the hedgeline on your right.

On your left is St George's Park and you will see among the new buildings the crucifix that tops the chapel of St George's Retreat (not accessible). Many Guild members, including Eric Gill, attended Mass in this chapel. Valentine KilBride and Susan Falkner's husband, Freddy, served Mass there on Sundays well into the 1970s. Two of the Pepler children, Susan and Stephen, were baptised at St George's. The former recalls being 'done' in the big font at the back of St George's Retreat Chapel. 'This was the bit reserved for the public where we normally went to Sunday Mass. We couldn't have Sunday Mass at the Guild chapel because the bishop wouldn't allow it. He disapproved of the whole set-up.' St George's Retreat is still a Roman Catholic convent; it was founded in 1866 by Augustinian nuns from Belgium who cared for the mentally ill. They have now developed a large retirement village and nursing home, St George's Park, which surrounds the original convent buildings.

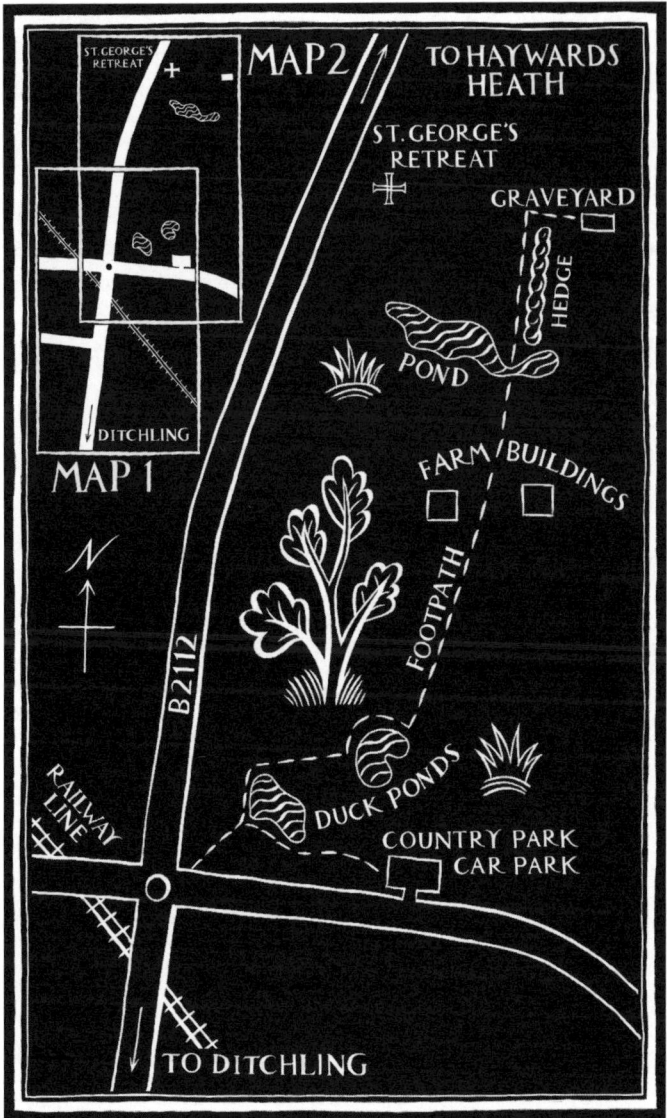

NB. *This map is not to scale.*

The footpath leads uphill and bends to the left round a group of trees. It crosses the private drive that leads from St George's to the graveyard. The St George's car park is to your left. Leaving the footpath, turn right onto the drive and walk through the landscaped gardens until you reach the walled graveyard. Enter this tranquil space and take a few minutes to enjoy the peace.

Two graves, carved by Joseph Cribb for Guild family members, are at the far end of the graveyard on the left hand wall. Mounted on the wall is the memorial to George Maxwell's son: 'Remember in your prayers Stephen Maxwell Carpenter in this guild and soldier in the Gordon Highlanders who died of wounds in Italy on January 12th 1944 aged 19 years.' This was originally on the wall of the Guild chapel.

Just to the right below is the grave of Valentine and Cecilia KilBride's young son, who died of meningitis. The stone reads: 'Anthony Charles KilBride Born Sept 9th 1927 Died May 24th 1929 With your crown you play in your simplicity Before the very altar of heaven.'

Return down the drive to where the footpath crosses and retrace your route back to the car park.

AROUND
ST MARGARET'S CHURCH
WALK 3

*'There is not one way of getting your living and
another way of saving your soul.'*

FATHER PATRICK BARDEN *WRITING ABOUT THE SPIRIT OF DITCHLING*

S
t Margaret's Church is home to several items made by artists
and craftsmen who have lived in and around the village at various
times and as such is a vibrant example of the lively integration of
creativity into village life. In many ways the church is the physical and
metaphorical heart of the village and this fruitful interaction between
artists and institution illustrates the close unity of the two. Here, art
is integral to the practices of everyday life, there is no separation between
the two. This visit takes approximately one hour.

St Margaret's Church

From the museum turn left and follow the gravel path around
towards the church, easily seen as it occupies an elevated position on a
sandstone knoll to the east. Climb the ramp and take the path through
the graveyard until you reach the South Porch of the church. (An
alternative route to the church on level ground is from Church Lane,
which is accessed from the High Street.) The Church of St Margaret of
Antioch dates from the late 12th century and is built on the site of an

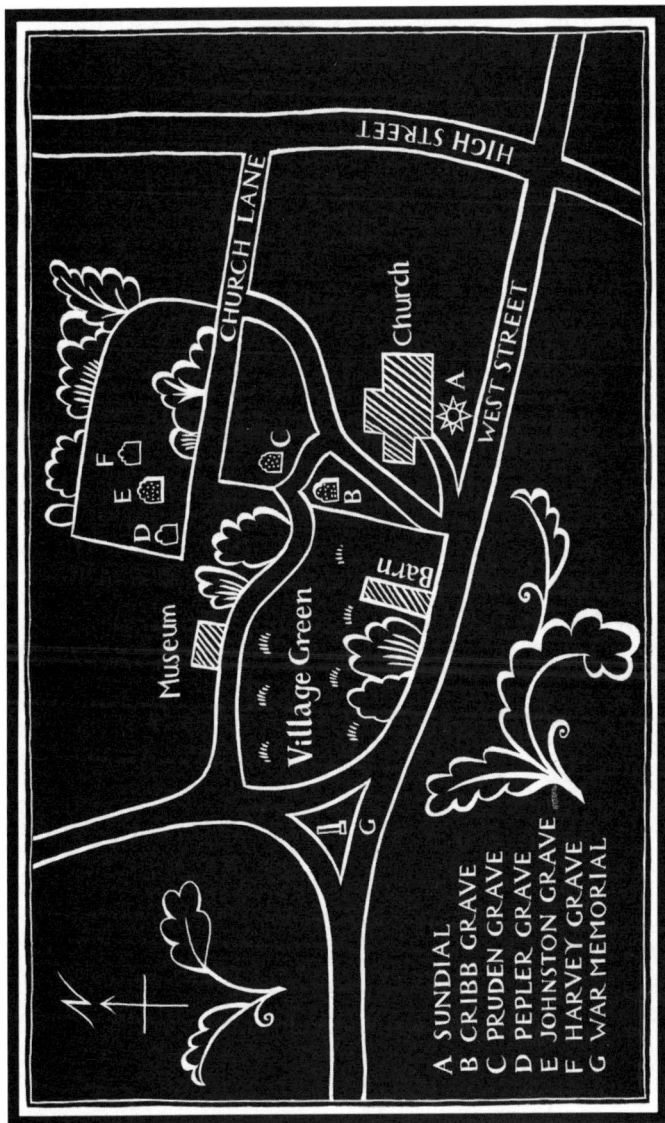

HIGH STREET

CHURCH LANE

Church

WEST STREET

C

F
E
D

B

A

Museum

Barn

Village Green

G

A SUNDIAL
B CRIBB GRAVE
C PRUDEN GRAVE
D PEPLER GRAVE
E JOHNSTON GRAVE
F HARVEY GRAVE
G WAR MEMORIAL

NB. *This map is not to scale.*

earlier Saxon church (remnants of this earlier structure are still visible in the west wall). The tower is later, dating from the late 13th or early 14th century. Note the use of sandstone tiles from Horsham (known as Horsham slab) that roof the porch and lower sections of the main roof. Caen stone, from Normandy, and flint (much of it knapped) have been used elsewhere.

Font

As you enter from the South Porch note the font, which lies immediately to your left. This striking piece, stark and beautiful in its simplicity, was carved by Gill's first apprentice and later assistant, Joseph Cribb.

West Door

Directly ahead on the left is the West Door. The two memorial curtains that hang at the door were woven by Hilary Bourne and it was she, along with her sister Joanna, who set up the original Ditchling Museum. Made of wool from Sussex flocks, the curtains show the natural undyed colours of fleece, with brown horizontal flecks and woven lettering. The left hand curtain reads 'In memory of Hilda Bourne for forty-six years member of this church who lived to be almost 103'. The other reads 'Spun by the Tree Spinners from wool of Sussex flocks and woven by her daughter Hilary Bourne'. The Tree Spinners were a local group of spinners and weavers, originally founded by Hilary Bourne and Marjorie Kenny. They used to meet in the garden shed of the house appropriately named Weavers, on the road to Clayton. This was home to Elizabeth Peacock, who was a well-known weaver in her own right and had been taught in Ditchling by Ethel Mairet at Gospels.

East Window

Walk along the nave towards the chancel. Above the altar is the East Window, designed by the artist Charles Knight in 1947. Its subject is the Lamb of God surrounded by doves of peace. In the wall to the left of the altar is an aumbry (recessed cupboard), decorated with a pelican; it was carved by Joseph Cribb.

Ten Commandments Tablet

Enter the 14th-century Abergavenny Chapel to your right and in the south-east corner is The Ten Commandments tablet. Like the font, this was also carved by Joseph Cribb and commissioned by Arthur Crookshank, the inspirational vicar who arrived at the parish in 1944. Numbered among Crookshank's many contributions to village life was the creation of the Village Association as well as the revival of the annual Village Pageant.

Ginnett Memorial

The oak screen that separates the Abergavenny Chapel from the South Transept was also carved by Joseph Cribb. Made c.1946 it was designed by John Denman, a Brighton architect, as a memorial to the artist Louis Ginnett. On each side at the centre are carvings of an artist's palette and brushes containing the initials LJG along with panels of daisies and oak and ivy leaves. The following is inscribed on the eastern face of the screen: 'To the memory of Louis John Ginnett, painter and designer, who lived for 28 years and died in this village on the 12th of August, 1946 aged 71 years', while on the western face it reads touchingly 'This screen, given by his widow, was designed and executed by his friends'.

Sundial

As you leave the church by the South Porch, bear to your left and find among the graves the small sundial. Carved on its south side is 'This was designed and cut by Gill' and 'Erected in commemoration of the coronation of King George V 57th monarch of England A.D.1911'.

Graveyard

The graveyard contains many stones that both commemorate and were carved by members and associates of the Guild of SS Joseph & Dominic. They may take a little finding among the long grass and wild flowers but are certainly worth the hunt.

Begin the search by retracing your footsteps back around the western side of the church. Note that a pathway from Church Lane intersects the graveyard, effectively cutting it in two; you are currently in the southern section. Search the row of stones on the far western boundary of the churchyard for Joseph Cribb's gravestone (to help you orientate, note that beyond the wall in front of you are the foundation stones of an old barn on the village green). This stone was made in Cribb's workshop by his assistant Kenneth Eager; it reads: 'Joseph Cribb sculptor 1892-1967 and his dear wife Mary Agnes 1898-1984 I will lift up mine eyes unto the hills.'

Now walk northwards towards the group of yew trees; underneath them is the grave of Dunstan Pruden. This is a flat stone rather than an erect one and reads, 'Dunstan Pruden Goldsmith 1906-1974 and his second wife Winefride who died on 18th February 2008 Rise, clasp my hand & come.'

Cross over the pathway from Church Lane to the most northern part of the graveyard. Note that just to the left of the gate that leads back towards the museum is the grave of the Pepler family. This fine stone was carved by Joseph Cribb; it reads: 'Hilary Douglas Clark Pepler 1877-1951 Claire Lilian Pepler 1880-1959 David Whiteman Pepler 1905-1934 Requiescant in pace.' Woodworkers from the Guild of SS Joseph & Dominic made Hilary Pepler's coffin and it was lined with cloth woven by Valentine KilBride. He was buried here following a Catholic Requiem Mass that was held in the Guild chapel on Ditchling Common.

A little further over to the east is the very fine stone commemorating the calligrapher Johnston and his wife, also carved by Cribb. The inscription reads, 'Edward Johnston 1872-1944 Greta Johnston 1872-1936 The peace of God which passeth all understanding be with you always.'

Just to the north of Johnston's stone is the grave of WWI soldier Walter Harvey. He served with the Royal Sussex Regiment and died at home in Lewes from wounds sustained in battle. His stone was designed and cut by Eric Gill and is in remarkably pristine condition: '318 Corporal Walter Harvey Royal Sussex Regiment 27th September 1917 Age 25.'

The Village Green

Retrace your footsteps back to the entrance to the churchyard and stand for a moment looking over the village green. Had it not been for the valiant efforts of a group of concerned villagers back in the 1960s, a housing estate would now replace the more bucolic scene before you. Originally the green and pond were all part of Ditchling Court Farm (the museum has several paintings that record the cowstalls, cart lodge and barns of the farmyard, most notably the 1940s watercolour by Charles Knight). In 1964 the Friends of Ditchling Charitable Trust was formed to oppose the threat of the site being sold to developers for housing and to create instead a village green. To help raise funds, one of the barns was sold to the East 15 Acting School in Loughton, Essex, where it was re-erected and used as a theatre (now known as the Harry Corbett Theatre). The foundations to this barn are still visible to your left. Beyond them lies another farm barn with a plaque commemorating the Queen's jubilee, carved by Gill's nephew John Skelton. The Grade II listed cart lodge to the right had stood empty since the 1960s but has now found an imaginative new use as the entrance to the Ditchling Museum of Art + Craft.

War Memorial

From the gate that leads towards the museum, turn left and walk towards West Street. Here you will find the war memorial. A fine, simple and fitting monument, it sits very well with the surrounding landscape. The memorial was carved at the Guild of SS Joseph & Dominic's stone-mason's workshop at Ditchling Common. Made of Portland stone and erected in 1920, the lettering was designed by Gill and cut by Joseph Cribb. The artist Louis Ginnett was chair of the committee that oversaw the creation of the village's memorial to the dead of WWI. Where possible, villagers were encouraged to donate sandstone blocks to surround the base of the memorial, what the local publication *The Beacon* called 'those large and curious stones which are to be found in royal and ancient town in old-world gardens and often at the corner of footpaths'. The names of those who fell in WWII were later added.

TO STREAT

WALK 4

*'The first principle in science is to invent something nice
to look at and then decide what it can do.'*

ROWLAND EMETT

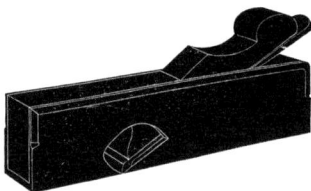

he walk to Streat is a pleasant stroll on the flat taking around
two hours there and back (it will take a little longer if you make
the detour to Stoneywish Nature Reserve). There are stiles to
climb. The main Ditchling figures featured on this walk are the sculptor
and lettercutter John Skelton and the inventor of weird and wonderful
machines Rowland Emett.

John Skelton was Eric Gill's nephew: his mother Angela, also known
as Margaret Evangeline, was Gill's youngest sister. Angela was the model
for Gill's large sculpture *Mankind*, which now forms part of the collection of London's Tate Gallery and was first known as *Humanity*. It depicts
the kneeling torso of a woman and was much praised. When first shown,
the critic PG Konody wrote, 'The rhythmic flow of the silhouette is
maintained from every point from which the torso is viewed; and the
sculptor's taste and technical skills have extracted from the Heptonwood
stone all the beauty of surface and texture which that material can
possibly yield.' John Skelton became Gill's assistant at Piggotts just four
months before his uncle's death in 1940; he then moved to Ditchling
to work with Joseph Cribb. Later he set up his own workshop in Streat
Lane and continued to live and work there until his death. His daughter,
Helen-Mary Skelton, still works from the premises.

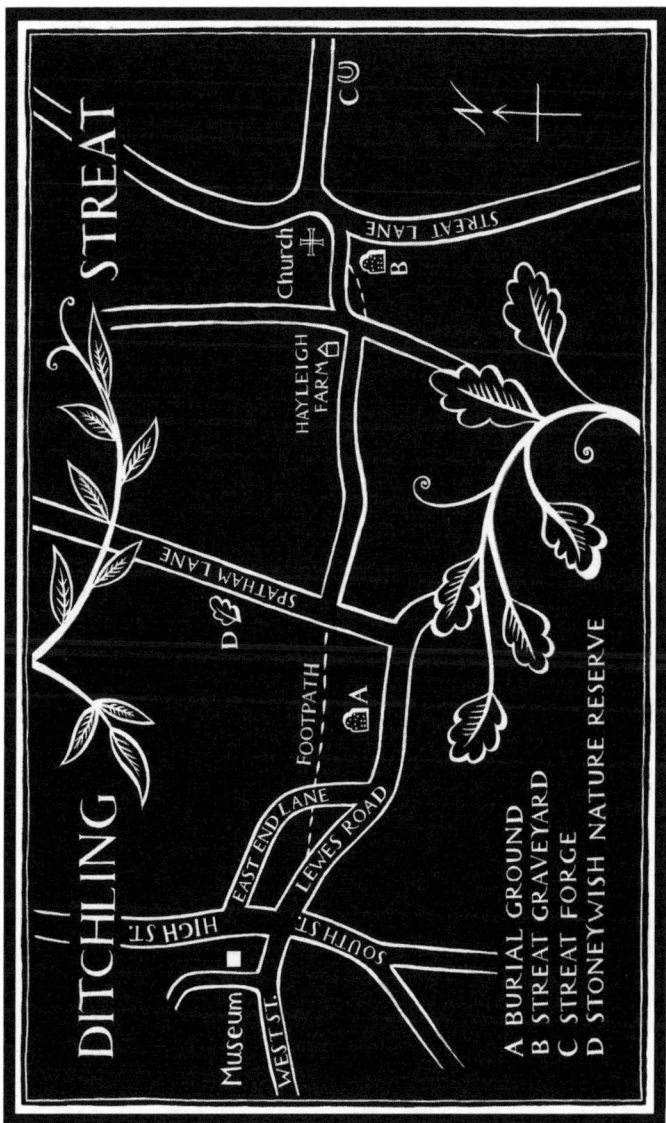

STREAT

DITCHLING

Church

STREAT LANE

HAYLEIGH FARM

SPATHAM LANE

FOOTPATH

EAST END LANE

LEWES ROAD

HIGH ST.

SOUTH ST.

WEST ST.

Museum

B

D

A

A BURIAL GROUND
B STREAT GRAVEYARD
C STREAT FORGE
D STONEYWISH NATURE RESERVE

NB. *This map is not to scale.*

Although Rowland Emett lived in Ditchling he also had a workshop in Streat, which he used when producing larger pieces. Many of the people who collaborated on his fantastical creations were craftsmen local to the area. There exists a charming film of Emett at work with one of his assistants in his garden at Wild Goose Cottage in Ditchling. To watch the 1963 film, called 'Cartoonist at Home', visit the website of British Pathé (*www.britishpathe.co.uk*).

Ditchling

From the museum turn left into West Street and continue until the road meets the junction with South Street and High Street. Cross into Lewes Road, staying on the left hand side of the road. Carry along a little way until you see The Fieldway on your left and a sign 'Footpath to Streat'.

Follow the footpath, crossing over East End Lane into Farm Lane. (Note that Rowland Emett's house, Wild Goose Cottage, is in East End Lane.) Carry on straight ahead, taking care not to follow the footpath sign just on the left as you enter Farm Lane. Go through the yellow metal gate, with tennis courts and a children's playground to your right. As the area opens out the rugby pitch is to your left and the cricket pitch is on the right. Bearing slightly to the left cross over the field and cross the small wooden bridge into the field used for football.

Burial Ground

As you enter the field the burial ground is on the right. Enter by the small wooden gate. The two graves of interest here are in the fourth and fifth rows of stones from the left. The most striking is the grave of the weaver Valentine KilBride, designed and carved by John Skelton. When he first came to Ditchling in 1924 KilBride worked as an assistant to Ethel Mairet, later becoming a member of the Guild of SS Joseph & Dominic. He and his wife Cecilia lived at Woodbarton on Ditchling Common. The KilBrides' grave is a tall slender stone and reads 'Pray for the soul of Valentine KilBride 1897-1982 Weaver and Dyer beloved of his wife Cecilia 1905-1985'. Note the inscription carved onto the edge of the stone: 'Anthony Clare Dominic Thomas Gilbert and Joanna.'

These are the names of the KilBride's six children (Joanna is now known as Jenny). Behind this stone slightly to the left is another KilBride family stone: 'Pray for the soul of Josephine KilBride 1892-1988.' Josephine was Valentine's sister and the stone was carved by Paul Wehrle, assistant to John Skelton.

Leave the burial ground and rejoin the path you were on that takes you across the field. Cross the stile and continue along this pleasant path planted with rhododendrons along your right hand side.

The path meets Spatham Lane. Cross over the road and follow the signpost for Streat. The route now follows a quiet tarmac road. As you pass by Hayleigh Farm to your left you need to cross over two stiles. You can now see Streat Church ahead.

Streat Church & Graveyard

After passing a few dwellings on your left you arrive at the church. Enter the graveyard on your right by the little gate. This is a particularly lovely spot and in spring the grass is carpeted with primroses. Orientate yourself with the war memorial to your left and head a little way into the graveyard to find two graves of note. The first belongs to Gill's nephew John Skelton. It reads 'John Skelton Sculptor & lettercutter 1923-1999' and was designed by his son Jonathan and daughter Helen Mary. The latter also carved the stone. On the ground in front of this stone is a lovely circular memorial that reads, 'Rebecca Alys Skelton Dancer. Choreographer. Teacher. Philosopher-Inspiring.' Rebecca Skelton (1968-2005) was Skelton's youngest daughter. Made of green Cumbrian stone, this too was designed by Rebecca's siblings and carved by Helen Mary. Following active service in WWII John Skelton worked for several years at Bridgeman's Monumental Masons in Lewes. He then set up a workshop with his wife in Burgess Hill. In 1958 they moved to a farmhouse called Blabers Mead in Streat, converting the stable block into a workshop. It is located at the southern end of Streat Lane and is quite a walk out of the village. His daughter Helen Mary Skelton still works there and runs various courses including sculpting and letter cutting (for details visit *www.skeltonworkshops.co.uk*).

Just behind Skelton's grave is that of Eric Gill's younger brother Max, marked by a gravestone by Joseph Cribb. This reads simply, 'MacDonald Gill 1884-1947'. Max Gill designed the first diagrammatic map of the London Underground and he also produced a highly illustrated version in 1914 called *Wonderground*. This map helped to improve the public's perception of the underground from a dirty and dark place to something altogether more jolly and inviting.

One of Max Gill's most important projects came from the War Graves Commission. They asked him to design letter forms to be used on the headstones of soldiers killed in action during WWI. Gill designed a Roman face, specifying that it be cut at a 60-degree angle (45 degrees was more usual) thus ensuring the names of the soldiers would resist the elements better and remain legible for decades to come. A new machine-cutting technique was employed in order to enable production of the shocking 180,000 stones that were needed to be made quickly. His brother Eric was rather disparaging about Max's work for the War Graves Commission, dismissing it as 'feebly artistic' and noting that good workmanship 'cannot be ordered, like coal, by the ton'. Perhaps the elder Gill thought that he, rather than his younger sibling, should have received this prestigious commission. Gill's assistant, Joseph Cribb, also worked in France for the War Graves Commission until 1919 after serving at the Somme in 1916-17. He surveyed and laid out war cemeteries and drew designs for the regimental badges that appeared on the graves.

Max Gill fell in love with Priscilla Johnston, Edward Johnston's daughter, and they eventually married in 1946 (for many years his first wife refused to grant him a divorce). They lived for many years in Priscilla's remote woodland cottage in West Sussex.

Streat Forge

Leave the churchyard, past the entrance to the church and Streat Place on the left. Cross Streat Lane into the little lane opposite. This is a private road, footpath and bridleway so please respect the privacy of the residents. Continue along until you reach Streat Forge on the right.

Now a private residence, this is the former workshop of Rowland Emett, inventor of Chitty Chitty Bang Bang and other fantastical machines, who was known locally as the 'Ditchling tinkerer' as it was thought that he tinkered about so much! Although Emett had a studio at his home in Ditchling, he also worked here at Streat Forge on his larger scale projects. He called it his 'secret forge' and somewhat cryptically commented that 'It's another shadow factory but the shadow falls in the opposite direction'. Emett's ambitious creations were in such demand that at one point he had 15 assistants working at the workshop.

The Emett Hut
Retrace your footsteps past the church and back to Spatham Lane. Instead of continuing on the footpath back to Ditchling, turn right and carry on a little way along the road, taking care of oncoming traffic. On the left is the entrance to Stoneywish Nature Reserve. Here you will find the charming Emett Hut Museum. The hut contains photographs, prints, designs and memorabilia relating to the life and work of Rowland Emett. Stoneywish is usually open March to October but the hut is not open every day so do please check opening times before you make this detour (visit *www.stoneywish.co.uk* or telephone 01273 843498). After your visit, turn right out of the main entrance to the nature reserve and walk along the road until you reach the sign for the footpath back to Ditchling, then continue on the same route back to the museum.

TO OLDLAND MILL

WALK 5

'Is heart aint where 'is body are, Tis out up on the downs.'
THE SUSSEX MAN, *LOUIS GINNETT*

O n this walk you will see two of the subjects painted by Charles Knight for the 1940s Recording Britain project: Oldland Mill and Ditchling Pond. Sir Kenneth Clark established the project shortly after the outbreak of war and its stated aim was 'Recording the changing face of Britain'. Not only was there a natural fear about the threat of bomb damage to the country but also anxiety about the rapidly changing appearance of the nation wrought by increased urbanisation, building development, new agricultural methods and loss of traditional skills. Funded by The Pilgrim Trust, Recording Britain commissioned many of the finest watercolourists of the day to produce drawings and paintings of vernacular architecture, churches, monuments and rural landscapes, all scenes that they felt typified the traditional British scene.

Ninety-seven artists produced over 1500 images for Recording Britain; many of these were shown at special exhibitions at London's National Gallery and then toured the country. The Victoria and Albert Museum now houses the complete collection. Ditchling was one of the first villages to be recorded in this way. Apart from the mill and pond, Knight painted many other locations in and around the village including Wick Farm, Lodge Barn and Anne of Cleves House (now known as Wings Place).

This is a relatively short walk (it takes no more than 45 minutes, although longer if you spend some time at the mill) with a very gentle

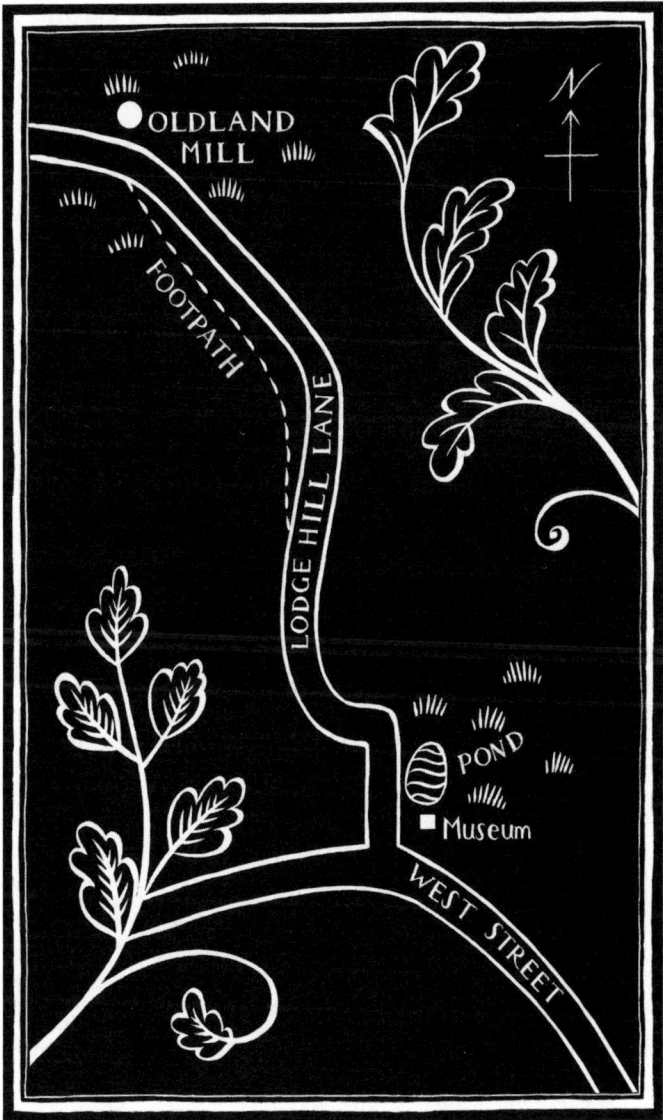

NB. *This map is not to scale.*

hill to climb and a couple of stiles to cross. Wellingtons are advisable in wet weather and binoculars useful as the views are far reaching.

Oldland Mill

From the museum turn right and continue along Lodge Hill Lane past the pond. The green mound rising before you is Lodge Hill, thought to be an ancient burial mound. The lane is a gentle climb and just after you reach the summit it turns into a bridleway (which can be extremely muddy during wet weather). Follow along until you reach Oldland Mill.

Oldland Mill is the oldest working mill in Sussex. Built in 1703, it was mentioned in 1755 in a Ditchling churchwarden's report but sadly was abandoned by 1912. The Sussex Archaeological Society was granted a lease on the mill in the 1920s by its owners, the Turner family. At that time it was estimated that £150 was needed to fund the restoration of the mill and in the 30s a 'shilling fund' was launched to raise the money. This effort failed, then in 1951 the artist Frank Brangwyn launched a second appeal to save the mill. This time the target was £500 but again it was unsuccessful. Windmills had long been a favourite subject for Brangwyn. A few years prior to his 1928 painting of Oldland Mill he had produced a book with Hayter Preston dedicated to the subject and simply called *Windmills*. Local artist Charles Knight produced several watercolours of Oldland Mill, including the one for the Recording Britain project.

After years of further deterioration, a lease for the mill was granted to the Hassocks Amenity Society in the early 1980s. A volunteer group was formed and a long programme of restoration began. A charity, the Oldland Mill Trust, was formed in 1997 and now runs the site. The work of the trust was rewarded in 2011 when the mill won a Sussex Heritage Award and the mill now grinds its own flour. Oldland Mill can be visited. It is usually open on the first Sunday of the month from April to October and volunteers work at the mill most Thursdays throughout the year but it is best to check dates and times for opening on their website *www.oldlandmill.co.uk*.

Having explored the mill, turn back towards the bridleway but instead of returning the way you came take the footpath slightly to the right. This route gives lovely views west towards Clayton. Keep to the path with the hedge on your left. You will find plenty of seats along the path where you can sit and enjoy the view. On the ridge of the Downs are two more windmills, the Clayton windmills, known locally as Jack and Jill. Like Oldland, Jill is a post mill while Jack is a tower mill. Eric Gill incorporated the three windmills you can see into his 1918 wooden-graving *View of Ditchling*, which he produced for the local Women's Institute. It was fitting for a windmill enthusiast such as Frank Brangwyn that Jack and Jill could be seen from the window of the room he referred to as his 'Sunday studio' at his home, The Jointure, in the village. He wrote, 'Man in his efforts to harness the forces of Nature has produced two beautiful wind-driven contrivances, the sailing ship and the windmill. The one defying the ungovernable fury of the sea; the other stemming the tide of the mighty wind with its frail fingers.'

Following the death of his first wife, Daisy Monica, in 1979, the artist Edgar Holloway often walked the route from his home in Keymer to Ditchling, walking up Lodge Hill to Oldland Mill. Among the many watercolours he painted of the area is *Keymer Bostall*, 1982. (A bostall is an ancient track.) He also produced several views of Lodge Hill Lane in the early 80s, and these very much convey the atmosphere of this tree-lined track.

Cross the stile and continue with the hedge to your left then cross another stile to rejoin Lodge Hill Lane and retrace the route back to the museum. As you approach the museum, note the view across the pond to the village green. Charles Knight also produced several watercolours of this view; again, some of these were for Recording Britain. When they were painted in the 1940s many more of the buildings belonging to Ditchling Court Farm still stood on the green.

UP ON THE DOWNS

WALK 6

*'The connection of my work [with Ditchling] is less to do with
Art and Culture and more to do with pubs.'*

RAYMOND BRIGGS

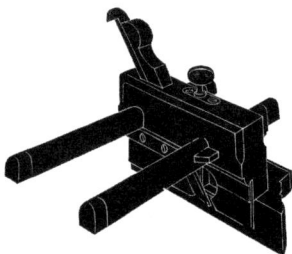

T he majestic presence of Ditchling Beacon has been the constant backdrop to the daily lives of all the artists and craftspeople who, over the years, have lived in and around the village. As well as offering recreation, the beacon was also a favourite subject for artists; most famously it was painted by Frank Brangwyn and Charles Knight but others too have sought to capture its ancient outline. More recently it has featured in the work of contemporary illustrators Raymond Briggs and John Vernon Lord.

Ditchling Beacon makes several appearances in the diaries of Eric Gill; 'Up the beacon with Ethel in eve' is a typical allusion. The Gill family, and their friends, were great walkers, and they would frequently stride out much further afield than the beacon. Gill and his children spent whole summer days tramping the Downs together. Setting out from the Jack and Jill windmills at Clayton, they would walk to Devil's Dyke, north of Brighton, then on to the Shepherd and Dog Inn at Fulking. Here Ethel would be waiting with the pony and trap and a hearty tea of boiled eggs, bread, butter and jam. The children then returned home with their mother while 'we elder ones would walk home

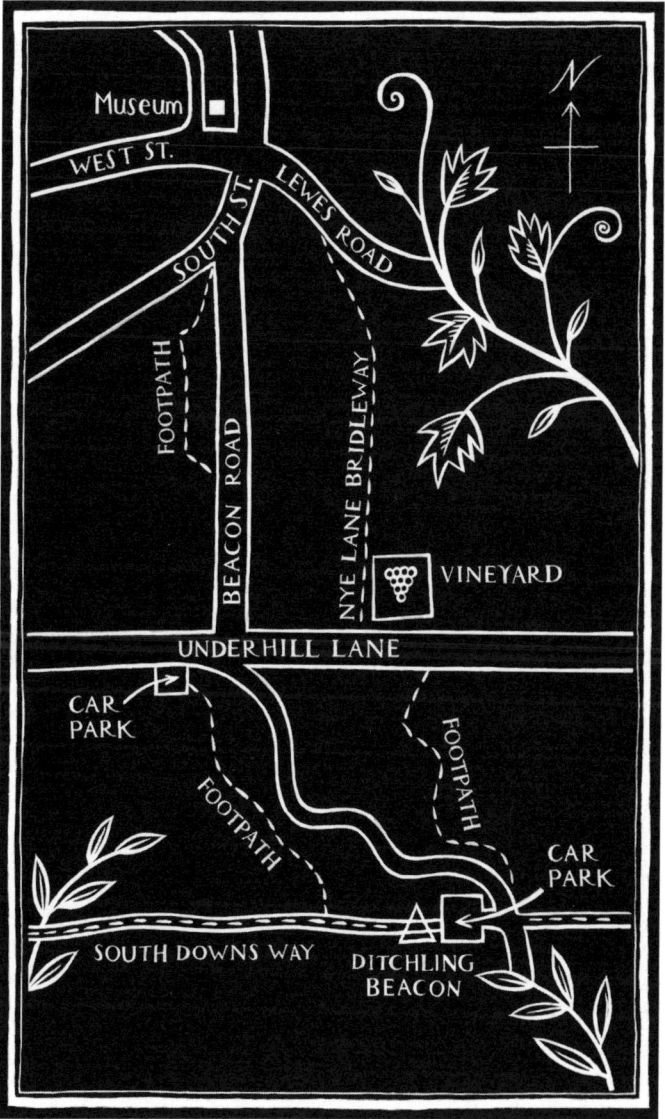

NB. *This map is not to scale.*

in the balmy beneficent evening under the Downs'. Years later, Gill remembered the impact this landscape had on him and his loved ones:

> If you have been a little child brought up in these hills and in those days, you
> will understand their mortal loveliness. If in your childhood, you have walked
> over them and in them and under them; if you have seen their sweeping roundness
> and the mists on them; and the sheep, and the little farmsteads in the bottoms,
> then you will know what I am talking about – but not otherwise. No one who
> was not there as a child can know that heaven, no grownup can capture it.

This walk follows a circular route approximately four miles long and it should take around an hour and a half, depending on walking pace. Inevitably it involves some uphill walking and climbing of stiles and it can be muddy in wet weather but the panoramic views it affords are well worth the effort.

Ditchling

Turn left from the museum and left again into West Street, then right into South Street, passing Frank Brangwyn's studio and his house, The Jointure, on the right. Where the road forks and South Street runs into Beacon Road, look for the signpost for the footpath just by the bench. Follow this path, with fences to each side, until you come to the housing estate. Follow the footpath sign, between the houses, then cross a stile and bridge into a field.

Turn left towards the line of the Downs, walking behind a row of gardens, then go through the small gap in the hedge. Continue along the path with the hedge on your left until you reach the corner of the field. Turn left and go through the gate. Follow the footpath straight ahead of you, crossing a small bridge. Follow the footpath, crossing another bridge, go through the gate and bear left. There is a metal gate and stile ahead. Cross this into Beacon Road. Turn right and follow the road (there is a grass footpath for most of the way although you will need to walk in the road for a little way). When you reach the crossroads you are in Underhill Lane.

Underhill Lane

Underhill Lane has been the home of writer and illustrator Raymond
Briggs for many years. Raymond told me the following amusing story
how he first came to live here and that the origins of his famous
story *The Snowman* are very much rooted in the area.

*My wife, Jean, and I moved to Burgess Hill from London in 1963 and we
found ourselves living near beautiful countryside and with the South Downs
only a few minutes' drive away.*

*Almost every day we drove through Ditchling then on up the hill to
Ditchling Beacon where we went for long walks. Later, we joined the Sussex
Downs Society (previously known as the Society of Sussex Downsmen. PC
strikes again! But quite rightly this time.) Coming down afterwards, we
always called in at Ditchling for a drink on the way home, usually at the
White Horse.*

*One day we were just coming near the bottom of the Beacon Hill when
I realised it was a Sunday. Oh heck! I said. The pubs don't open till seven,
dammit. It's only half past six. We can't hang about outside waiting, let's
turn down here. It'll pass the time. So we turned right into Underhill Lane
where we had never been before.*

*For some time we had been thinking of moving house, so when we saw a
FOR SALE sign outside a small bungalow we stopped to look at it.*

*It was tiny, just one door and one window. The house was hopeless, we
agreed, but what a position! Right at the foot of the downs. Nothing between
it and the beacon. Bound to cost a fortune.*

*But it turned out to be the colossal sum of £5,400, which we could just
about afford with a mortgage and the sale of our house for £4,500. Later,
after looking inside, we stood on the front doorstep gazing out over 26 miles
of the Sussex Weald to Ashdown Forest. Blimey! We later discovered that the
house was exactly on the 300 foot contour line. Quite high up, not at the
bottom of the hill.*

*The long arm of Coincidence strikes again! The Church still telling us
what to do with our leisure time, or rather when they would allow us to
do it, and so because of those antiquated Church laws about pubs' opening*

hours, we found a house. And 49 years later, we are still there, or more correctly, I am.

The main effect on my work, I suppose, was that the Snowman in my book was built in the garden here, he then flies over Ditchling Beacon and the downs to Brighton where he lands on the pier. There he is awe-struck by the sight of the rising sun, so he and the boy fly back to the garden. There, they hug one another goodnight, the boy goes indoors to bed and the Snowman stands awaiting his fate.

So the decaying powers of the C of E and the opening hours of the White Horse pub in Ditchling determined where I've been living for the last half century.

Ditchling Beacon

Once in Underhill Lane, cross the road to the small car park on the right. The footpath that goes up to the beacon lies ahead. Cross the stile and follow the steep path uphill. After crossing the next stile take the left fork up the chalky slope. Carry on along the path, keeping the chalk quarry to your left.

After levelling out, the path descends then turns right then finally up to the top of the ridge. The path opens out into a field. Bear left and follow the South Downs Way, climbing slightly until you reach Ditchling Beacon. Now draw breath to enjoy the spectacular views!

At 813 feet above sea level the Beacon is one of the highest points along the length of the South Downs. Perhaps the most iconic painting of Ditchling Beacon is the 1938 oil by Charles Knight (now in the collection of the Towner in Eastbourne). Penny Johnston has written eloquently of this work:

Anyone familiar with the scenery of the South Downs will know the distinctive profile of where the Downs meet the sky and appreciate how well Charles Knight has captured this aspect of Ditchling Beacon. He has also caught the particular glow of light that is seen here at the end of the afternoon in late summer and the way the shadows are cast in the hollow of the hills. Here is a painting that combines the feeling

of permanence in the presence of the Downs with that of the transitory
nature of the sky and the reflections in the water. These qualities
make this a compelling painting for me and is one of the most successful
evocations of the South Downs that I have seen.

Knight moved to Ditchling in 1934 and lived at 34 Beacon Road in a house called Chettles (not now visible from the road). He quickly adapted to rural life and during the war kept goats for milk. Knight would walk the surrounding landscape searching out subjects for his paintings and drawings (he produced 40 drawings of Sussex for the Recording Britain project alone). As he did not drive, his wife, Leonora, would often take him in the car to locations further afield, or he would catch local transport. In the autumn of 1939 Knight became very active in a national campaign to halt the proposed unregulated speculative development of the stretch of land at the base of the Downs from Ditchling to Keymer. It is fortunate for us all that the campaign was a success.

Stay on the track until you reach the National Trust Car Park. Go through the car park to the road, turn left and head down the grass verge then cross the road and follow the fence, keeping to the bridleway with the fence to your right. Carry on, now with ash trees to your right, then through trees and bushes. When the path rejoins Underhill Lane, turn left and walk a little way along until you reach Nye Lane Bridleway on the right.

Take the bridleway, passing Ditchling Vineyard on the right, and continue along. The path becomes a concrete drive and bears to the left but keep going straight ahead. There is a stretch of woodland to your left. Carry on until you reach a marker and follow the direction of the blue arrow. A little way along is another blue marker indicating your route to the right. Follow this path a little further. Cross the stile, follow the path, then cross another stile. Now walk diagonally to the left and across the field. You can see St Margaret's Church ahead, in an elevated position above the village. Carry on in the same direction across the next two fields, again climbing another two stiles. Follow the lane, walking between hedges and houses, until you reach Lewes Road. Head left towards the crossroads and back along West Street to the museum.

Before you turn right into Lodge Hill Lane from West Street, look at the house called Wings Place on the left. This Grade I listed timber-framed Elizabethan house was aptly described by Nikolaus Pevsner as 'eminently picturesque in a water-colourist's way' and indeed it has been painted many, many times. Even Eric Gill depicted it in a childhood watercolour. It also puts in an appearance in the much-loved children's book *The Giant Jam Sandwich* by John Vernon Lord. A local resident since 1971, Lord often draws inspiration from the quirkier buildings that can be found around the village, along with the delights of the surrounding countryside. Ditchling (including Wing's Place) was the model for the background scenes in Lord's 1989 edition of *Aesop's Fables*.

THE BIOGRAPHIES

Joanna Bourne 1906-91 *Writer & Editor*
Hilary Bourne 1909-2004 *Weaver*
Marjorie Bourne 1904-89 *Teacher*

The Bourne sisters were born in India but following the death of her husband their mother, Hilda, moved the family to England. Once in Ditchling the girls boarded at North End House School (later known as Dumbrells). Edward Johnston taught Marjorie calligraphy. As a young woman Hilary travelled to Palestine, where she learnt to weave. On her return she worked with Muriel Rose at The Little Gallery in London, which sold work by Ethel Mairet, Bernard Leach and Shoji Hamada. During WWII she worked with Mairet, later producing curtains for London's Royal Festival Hall. Her woven fabrics were used to furnish passenger planes. Other works included early woven lurex and even fabric used for costumes worn by Charlton Heston in the film *Ben Hur*. Joanna read French at Oxford and later taught at North End House School, along with her sister Marjorie. The sisters were very active in acquiring works by members of the Guild of SS Joseph & Dominic and in 1985, when both were in their 70s, Joanna and Hilary opened the original Ditchling Museum, which housed an eclectic mix of fine examples of Guild craftsmanship set alongside folk and country items.

Sir Frank Brangwyn 1867-1956 *Artist*

Born in Bruges, Belgium, where Brangwyn's architect father was working, the family returned to London when Frank was aged eight. With little or no formal art training, Brangwyn worked briefly for William Morris. He had a precocious talent for painting and exhibited at the Royal Academy in 1885, aged only 18. Following a period of travel he quickly gained a reputation for sea and landscapes and his work was in demand at home and abroad. Along with large-scale paintings, Brangwyn produced many decorative murals and friezes. He also produced etchings, lithographs, woodcuts, along with designs for furniture, textiles, ceramics, metalwork and glass.

In 1918 Brangwyn and his wife, Lucy, bought the house and studio known as The Jointure in Ditchling. She died in the early 20s but Brangwyn kept the house and he eventually died there aged 89. Although he had known Gill, Pepler and Johnston in the Hammersmith days, he never became a member of the Guild of SS Joseph & Dominic.

In 1926 Brangwyn was commissioned to produce a series of large murals for the north and south walls of the House of Lords' Royal Gallery as a memorial to peers and their family members lost in WWI. Brangwyn's original plan featured realistic battle scenes but, following two years' work, these were rejected by Lord Iveagh, who was funding the project. By 1930 Brangwyn had produced the British Empire Panels depicting scenes from the dominions and colonies that had fought for Britain in the war. Again these were rejected, this time by the Royal Fine Arts Commission, and despite vigorous support for the works from influential quarters the Lords voted against the scheme. This was a bitter blow indeed for Brangwyn (the panels are now on display in the Guildhall, Swansea).

Brangwyn was knighted in 1941 and the Royal Academy staged a retrospective of his work in 1952, the first living artist to be thus honoured. Despite this success, his latter years were marred by his belief that he and his work were out of step with the direction of modern art.

Raymond Briggs b.1934 *Illustrator & Writer*
A long time resident of the area, Briggs was born in London and studied at Wimbledon Art School and the Central School of Art then, following National Service, the Slade School of Art. His published work as a graphic artist is prolific and includes such classic titles as *The Snowman*, *Father Christmas*, *Fungus the Bogeyman* and *When the Wind Blows*. The Kate Greenaway Medal and the British Book Awards Children's Book of the Year are among the numerous awards he has won over the years. As well as working as an illustrator, Briggs taught part time at Brighton College of Art alongside John Vernon Lord. Still working, Briggs also contributes a regular column to *The Oldie* magazine, a compilation of which was published in 2015, entitled *Notes From the Sofa*.

Lawrence Christie 1872-1941 *Artist & Calligrapher*
A pupil of Edward Johnston, Christie went briefly into partnership with
Gill when they were both in London. He later moved to Ditchling and
lived at Crossways and Rowlescroft.

Desmond Chute 1895-1957 *Engraver & Priest*
Desmond Macready Chute had briefly studied at the Slade School of
Art then met Gill in 1918 while the latter was working on the Stations
of the Cross for Westminster Cathedral. A Catholic, he visited Gill at
Ditchling Common and quickly joined the family as an apprentice stone
carver. Chute had a close working relationship with Gill and was so
trusted that he was left in charge of the workshops when Gill was called,
briefly, for war service. He also worked alongside Gill on the Stations
of the Cross at St Cuthbert's, Bradford. After he left Ditchling he studied
for ordination at the Albertinum, Fribourg, Switzerland and then served
as a priest at Rapallo in Italy.

Ewan Clayton b.1956 *Calligrapher*
The grandson of Valentine KilBride, Clayton was the last member to
join the Guild of SS Joseph & Dominic, in 1982. An internationally
acclaimed calligrapher, he is author of *The Golden Thread: A History
of Writing*.

Joseph Cribb 1892-1967 *Sculptor, Carver & Lettercutter*
Cribb was 14 when he became Gill's first assistant at his London
workshop in Hammersmith in 1906. He came with Gill to Ditchling in
1907 and was his first apprentice 1908-13. Many examples of his work
are evident in the village. Influenced by his mentor's conversion from
nonconformism to the Roman Church, Cribb also became a Catholic
in 1913. After Gill left Ditchling for Wales, Cribb ran the stonemason's
workshop on Ditchling Common, specialising in gravestones, inscriptions and devotional carvings, especially for churches. He continued to
collaborate with Gill on many works and remained prolific until he died
in Folders Lane on his way to work.

John Denman 1882-1975 *Architect*

Denman ran a very busy architectural practice in Brighton and also taught at Brighton School of Art, eventually becoming head of the architecture department. Charles Knight was one of his pupils. He designed the two stone pylons that originally stood either side of the London Road at Patcham outside Brighton (the road was then narrower than it is today) and it is thought that Louis Ginnett worked with him on this project. He collaborated with Joseph Cribb on many commissions and was friends with many of the craftsmen of the Guild of SS Joseph & Dominic.

Rowland Emett OBE 1906-90 *Cartoonist, Sculptor & Inventor*

Born in London, Emett was a commercial artist until WWII when he worked as a draughtsman for the Air Ministry. After the war he became a regular contributor to *Punch*, producing drawings of fantasy trains. For the 1951 Festival of Britain, Emett's designs for the steam engines Nellie, Neptune and Wild Goose leapt from the page to become life-size creations made of beaten copper and mahogany. They were an instant success with Festival visitors.

Emett's inventions and creations, which he called his 'things', were much in demand and commissions from companies such as Shell and Featherstone followed. He designed the car Chitty Chitty Bang Bang for the 1968 film of the same name. He also had a travelling show called Emettland, which toured all over the world. He and his wife, Mary, moved to Wild Goose Cottage in Ditchling, where he had a studio. He also produced large-scale pieces at a forge in Streat, where he employed as many as 15 assistants. His many publications include *Engines, Aunties, and Others* (1943), *The Early Milk Train* (1976) and *Emett's Ministry of Transport* (1981).

Sir Jacob Epstein 1880-1959 *Sculptor*

Born in New York, Epstein moved to London in 1905, becoming a British citizen some years later. He was at the forefront of modern art in the first half of the 20th century, producing many major, often contentious, public works. He worked with Gill during the early years at Ditchling. He was knighted in 1954.

Eric Gill 1882-1940 *Sculptor, Artist, Typographer & Writer*
Born at 32 Hamilton Road in Brighton, Gill was the second child of the Reverend Arthur Tidman Gill and his wife, Rose. In 1897 his father attended the Chichester Theological College and began to move away from his Dissenters background towards the more mainstream Church of England. Eric was 14 when the family moved to 2 North Walls, close to Chichester Cathedral. Fiona MacCarthy has written about the importance of this period for the young Gill, commenting that the city was 'a lasting symbol of perfection, the ideal of the good city, human, decorous, coherent. The vision of Chichester always remained central to Gill's passionate urge to achieve an integration of life, art, work and worship, his sense of his own mission – often thwarted – "to make a cell of good living in the chaos of our world".' It was also at Chichester that Gill first developed his interest in lettering, when he attended the Technical and Art School.

Aged 18, he moved to London to study architecture at the office of WD Caroe, a practice that mainly dealt with ecclesiastical work. In 1902 he met the Arts & Crafts calligrapher Edward Johnston. He also began to attend evening classes in practical masonary at Westminster Technical Institute and in lettering and illumination at the Central School of Arts & Crafts (where Johnston taught). He also began to lodge at Johnston's chambers at Lincoln's Inn, becoming a pupil and disciple of the revered calligrapher. Fabian socialism, craft guilds, craftsmen's communities, back-to-the-landers, all were prevalent ideologies at this time and had a profound influence on the young Gill.

Once Gill's stone carving talents began to be evident he started to get commissions for tombstones, ecclesiastical inscriptions and letter cutting, both for Caroe and other architectural practices. This prompted him to set up on his own, carving and painting signs (including for the stationers WH Smith). In 1904 Gill married Ethel Moore (1878-1961) whom he had met at Chichester (her father was the head verger of the Cathedral) and they set up home in the London suburb of Battersea, in what he called the 'enchanted garden of Christian marriage'. Their first child, Betty, was born the following year and they moved to Hammersmith, where Johnston and his wife were already living. Hilary Pepler and his wife also lived in the area. Gill turned the stable building next to their cottage into a workshop and employed his first assistant, Joseph Cribb, and they worked together carving inscriptions and memorial stones.

In 1907 Gill, Ethel and their two younger daughters moved to the East Sussex village of Ditchling, renting a house in the High Street called Sopers. An outhouse was converted into a workshop and he wrote, 'I'm doing all sorts of lettering for a living and between times writing, arguing, preaching, jawing, persuading anybody who cares that good construction is the only thing that can be taught or talked about.' From 1909 Gill began to create free-standing stone sculptures, and he took part in a critically acclaimed exhibition at Chenil Gallery, Chelsea, London in 1911.

In 1913 Gill and his wife converted to Catholicism (Ethel changing her name to Mary) and moved into a house called Hopkins Crank at Ditchling Common. They now had three daughters. Gill set up a series of workshops on the Common and undertook several high profile commissions, including the Stations of the Cross for London's Westminster Cathedral. (This exempted him from military service for most of the war and he was not called up until September 1918.) During this period Pepler set up St Dominic's Press, for which Gill wrote pamphlets and produced wood engravings.

Many of Gill's most ardent admirers had followed him when he left the village and the years on Ditchling Common were characterised by increasing religious fervour; Gill joined the Third Order of St Dominic, a lay order of the Dominicans, and designed and built a chapel behind his house, as well as workshops and houses. In 1920 he and Pepler, with Desmond Chute and Joseph Cribb, founded the craft Guild of SS Joseph & Dominic. Of its aims he wrote, 'The love of God means that work must be done according to an absolute standard of reasonableness; the love of our neighbour means that work must be done to an absolute standard of serviceableness. Good quality is therefore twofold, work must be good in itself and good for use.' St Dominic's Press published books and pamphlets that made the ideals of the Guild available to a wider audience, thus further attracting new members. By 1922 there were 41 Catholics living and working at the Guild, mostly on land owned by Pepler.

The idyll, however, was not to last. There were increasing tensions, both financial and personal, between Gill and other Guild members, in particular with Pepler. Concentrated periods of work became difficult due to the almost continual stream of visitors and admirers. Gill both sought publicity yet yearned to escape it. One visitor to the Guild, Donald Attwater, told Gill about some deserted monastic buildings he knew of at Capel-y-ffin in the Llanthony Valley, Wales, and these became the focus for Gill's desire to leave Ditchling and all its tensions. On 22 July 1924 Gill formally resigned from the Guild of SS Joseph & Dominic and in August he and his family left for the Welsh hills. The rift between him and Pepler was never properly healed. The Gills then left Capel-y-ffin in 1928, moving to Piggots, close to High Wycombe in Buckinghamshire.

Throughout his life Gill worked tirelessly on a great range of commissions and created some of the most influential and widely used modern typefaces. He died in October 1940 aged only 58 and is buried at Speen in Buckinghamshire. His gravestone was cut by Laurie Cribb (who was Gill's main assistant from 1925, replacing his brother Joseph) and bears the legend 'Pray for me Eric Gill 1882-1940 and for my most dear wife Mary Gill 1878-1961'.

Louis Ginnett 1875-1946 *Artist*

Although he was never a member of the Guild of SS Joseph & Dominic, Ginnett spent many years living in Ditchling. He painted portraits, murals and interiors as well as designing stained glass. He also taught at Brighton College of Art and his pupils included the painter Charles Knight, who later became his friend.

Philip Hagreen 1890-1988 *Wood Engraver & Writer*

Born in Crowthorne, Berkshire, Hagreen studied with the Newlyn School of painters and later at the New Cross Art School and at Heatherleys in London. A convert to Catholicism, by 1915 Hagreen was already an important figure in the Catholic craft revival of the early years of the 20th century. In 1924 he went to work as a lettercutter to Gill in Ditchling, of whom he said 'He used his friends as whet stones on which to sharpen his ideas'. Later in 1924 Hagreen went with Gill to Capel-y-ffin in Wales for a brief time. The harsh conditions and enforced intimacy, along with his poor health, put a strain on the relationship between the two men and he soon left, although they remained friends. Gill had a lasting influence on Hagreen, whom he had met when they both became founder members of The Society of Wood Engravers in 1920 (other founder members were Robert Gibbings, John Nash, Lucien Pissarro, Gwen Raverat and Noel Rooke).

Hagreen moved to France but continued producing illustrations for Pepler's St Dominic's Press. In 1930 he returned to Ditchling, working at the Guild until 1955. He carved in wood and ivory and produced many fine illustrations and examples of lettering, both as woodcuts and engravings. He was a prolific writer of letters, articles and poetry, and also taught at Brighton College of Art. Hagreen worked for many small printing presses; among his illustrative work is *Silversmithing* by Dunstan Pruden. He was married to Aileen Mary Clegg, a writer.

Edgar Holloway 1924-2008 *Artist, Etcher, Letterer & Designer*

Born in Yorkshire, Holloway displayed a precocious talent for etching when very young. Many of his early works were acquired by the Victoria and Albert Museum and the British Museum and he produced portraits of several famous sitters. A Catholic convert, Holloway met and married Gill's former model Daisy Monica Hawkins at Capel-y-ffin. He joined the Guild of SS Joseph & Dominic in 1950 at the invitation of Philip Hagreen. For the first four years that he was at the Guild he lived at the Old School House, formerly used as a laundry, and later moved to St Rose in Fragbarrow Lane. Following the death of his first wife, Holloway married Jennifer Boxall and they moved into Woodbarton Cottage on Ditchling Common. He was the chairman of the Guild when it closed in 1989.

Edward Johnston CBE 1872-1944 *Calligrapher, Teacher & Writer*
Johnston was born in Uruguay into a military family; they returned to the UK when Edward was aged three. Johnston originally studied medicine in Edinburgh but then developed a keen interest in letter forms. He moved to London where he met WR Lethaby, then principal of the Central School of Arts & Crafts. He urged Johnston to study early and medieval manuscripts. This resulted in a chance meeting with Sidney Cockerell in the British Museum Manuscript Room, which proved influential. Johnston wrote passionately that he felt his life's work was 'to make *living letters* with a formal pen'. He married Greta Greig (1872-1936) in 1902 and they lodged at Lincoln's Inn and Hammersmith. At Lethaby's request he taught calligraphy at the Central School (as well as the Royal College of Art), where Gill became his pupil. A close friendship developed between the two and Gill lodged for a time at Johnston's chambers in Lincoln's Inn. In 1906 he published the extremely influential handbook *Writing & Illuminating, & Lettering*.

The Johnstons moved to Ditchling in 1912, living on the Common between 1912 and 1920 before returning to the village. Neither Edward nor Greta shared Gill's passionate Catholicism. He was also uncomfortable with Father Vincent McNabb's Catholic vision for the Guild and avoided becoming a member.

Today Johnston is best known for the sans serif typeface and the famous roundel that he designed for the London Underground, collaborating with Gill on the early designs.

David Jones 1895-1975 *Poet, Writer & Painter*
Jones had seen active service in WWI and following demobilisation he studied at Westminster School of Art. He first visited Ditchling Common in 1921. Like many young men damaged by the war, Jones was drawn to Gill and his seemingly Utopian community at the Guild. He

converted to Catholicism during his first year at the Guild and stayed at the cottage in the paddock on the Common known as The Sorrowful Mysteries. Here he painted the mural *Floribus et Palmis* illustrating the entry of Jesus into Jerusalem. As a member of the Guild he learnt wood engraving and carving along with calligraphy (a skill he fully exploited in his 1952 work *The Anathemata*). Jones became a postulant of the Order of St Dominic. For a short time he was engaged to Gill's middle daughter, Petra. In 1924 he painted a symbolic picture called *The Garden Enclosed* (Tate Britain) depicting young lovers in the garden at Hopkins Crank.

Jenny KilBride MBE b.1948 *Weaver*

As the daughter of Valentine and Cecilia KilBride, Jenny KilBride was brought up among members of the Guild of SS Joseph & Dominic on Ditchling Common. KilBride returned to Ditchling in 1972 to work with her father and in 1974 became the first woman to join the Guild (interestingly there were only ever two female members, the silversmith Winefride Pruden being the other). Following the winding up of the Guild in 1989 KilBride worked at Glyndebourne Opera House. As a Trustee of the museum at Ditchling, KilBride was extremely influential and effective in raising funds and generating momentum for the creation of the new Ditchling Museum of Art + Craft.

Valentine KilBride 1897-1982 *Silk Weaver & Vestment Maker*

Born in Bradford, Yorkshire, KilBride served in the Navy in WWI. He was greatly influenced by writers such as Hilaire Belloc and GK Chesterton, although William Morris had the most profound effect, leading him to believe that 'a peasantry and an industry of craftsmen were the answers to the social problems of our time'. After training as a handloom weaver, KilBride arrived at Ditchling in 1924 and became assistant to Ethel Mairet at Gospels. He joined the Guild of SS Joseph & Dominic in 1926 and set up his workshop, specialising in weaving silk and making church vestments. He continued working at the Guild until his death in 1982.

Charles Knight 1901-90 *Painter & Lecturer*

Knight was born and grew up in Brighton, remaining a resident of Sussex all his life. He studied at Brighton School of Art from 1919 to 1923, then at the Royal Academy Schools in London. Both Louis Ginnett and John Denman taught Knight at Brighton and later became his friends when he returned as a tutor. He and his wife, Leonora, moved to Ditchling in 1934. She had also studied at Brighton School of Art and worked as a commercial artist and as a sculptor. They first rented then later bought a house called Chettles, located at 34 Beacon Road (not visible from the road). Both were much involved in village life; Knight was a Server and Church Warden at St Margaret's.

Knight exhibited regularly both locally and in London and became an associate of the Royal Society of Painters in Watercolour. He also produced a series of popular inn signs for Brighton's Kemp Town Brewery. In the early 1940s the Ministry of Labour instigated a scheme called Recording Britain. Its aim was to record for posterity a Britain then perceived to be under threat from both foreign invasion and unprecedented industrial and social change. Knight was commissioned to record Ditchling (one of the first places to be selected for the project) along with other Sussex sites further afield.

The oil *Ditchling Beacon* (Towner Art Gallery, Eastbourne), painted by Knight in 1938, is one of the most iconic views of the South Downs ever produced, and among his prolific output are numerous Sussex scenes, many in or very close to Ditchling itself. Sadly, Knight was forced to leave Chettles in October 1987, following damage wreaked by the Great Storm. He spent his last days at the Rosemount Nursing Home in nearby Hassocks.

Bernard Leach 1887-1979 *Potter & Writer*

Leach studied briefly at the Slade School of Fine Art in London then later at the London School of Art. It was there that he met Frank Brangwyn. As well as teaching him etching, Brangwyn schooled Leach in his ideas about art and craft and shared his enthusiasm for Japanese art and culture. Leach had spent his early years in Japan and it was there that he first began to work as a potter. He arrived back in England in 1920 along with the Japanese potter Shoji Hamada and set up the Leach Pottery in St Ives, Cornwall. In 1921 Leach and Hamada visited Ethel Mairet and the community at Ditchling Common. Hamada was so influenced by this experience that he later set up a similar artists' community in Mashiko, Japan. Leach returned to Ditchling in the mid 1930s and lived for a time in a caravan with his wife and dog on the Downs outside the village. He made several sepia sketches of the local area at this time.

John Vernon Lord b.1939 *Author, Illustrator & Lecturer*

Born in the Peak District of Derbyshire, Lord moved south to Sussex to teach illustration at Brighton College of Art (now the University of Brighton) in the 1960s. Alongside his long and distinguished teaching career, Lord continued to work as a prolific illustrator. After moving to Ditchling (where he still lives with his wife, Denie) in the 1970s, the village and its environs began to feature in many of his books, most notably *The Giant Jam Sandwich* and *Aesop's Fables*. Still as productive as ever, Lord finds that the area continues to be a source of inspiration to him today.

Ethel Mairet 1872-1952 *Weaver, Dyer & Writer*

Ethel Partridge was born in Barnstaple, Devon and in her early career worked briefly as a governess. Her first husband was the art historian, critic and philosopher Ananda Coomaraswamy. A geologist from Ceylon, Coomaraswamy became an expert on the Arts & Crafts of India and had a profound influence on Gill, especially his theories concerning the sacred nature of sensual art. Gill wrote the preface to Coomaraswamy's 1914 book *Visvakarma*, stating, 'The whole business of art is entirely without importance except in so far as it is conceived and conducted as the material expression of religion.' The Coomaraswamys travelled to Ceylon (now Sri Lanka) and India, where they studied and collected native Arts & Crafts and where Ethel first learned the craft of hand-weaving. After their divorce in 1912 she moved to Ditchling and in 1913 met and married her second husband, Philip Mairet (1886-1975), writer, philosopher, ecologist and actor. During WWI he worked as a farm hand at the Pepler's farm on Ditchling Common.

Ethel experimented with weaving and dyeing techniques using natural dyes. She published an influential treatise, *A Book on Vegetable Dyes*, in 1916. It was one of the earliest books published by Pepler's St Dominic's Press. The same year, she and Philip moved to Ditchling. They built a home and workshop, Gospels, in the village. Here she took in apprentices, including Petra Gill, and produced simple and natural cloth that sold well. She taught her craft zealously, including at Brighton College of Art, and was the first woman to be honoured by the Royal Society of Arts. Such was her international reputation that Mahatma Gandi met with her on a visit to London and sought her advice on his project of running spinning and weaving workshops in Indian villages. The Mairets divorced in 1931 and Ethel remained at Gospels for the rest of her life. She is buried at Dyke Road Cemetery, Brighton.

George Maxwell 1890-1957 *Carpenter*
Maxwell came to Ditchling from Birmingham in 1922 to join the Guild. His workshop specialised in high quality furniture, church fittings and looms. He was also responsible for the erection, to designs by Gill, of many of the Guild buildings on Ditchling Common. After WWII he was joined by his son John, who continued to run the workshop after his father's death.

Frank Partridge 1871-1952 *Jeweller, Silversmith, Wood & Metal Worker*
Brother of Ethel Mairet, Partridge lived and worked at Ditchling.

Arthur Penty 1875-1937 *Architect*
Penty wrote on socialism, distributism and the model of the medieval guild system and associated with members of the Guild of SS Joseph & Dominic. He lived for a time at Ditchling in Hillway House, which he designed.

Hilary Pepler 1878-1951

Publisher, Printer, Writer, Social Reformer & Puppeteer

Originally known as Douglas, Pepler was born in Eastbourne, East Sussex. He married Claire Whiteman (1876-1960), a painter, in 1904, moving to Hammersmith the following year. Edward Johnston was a close friend and neighbour and it was at Johnston's home that Pepler first met Gill. Pepler's daughter Susan Falkner recounts how her father 'and Johnston and Gill used to meet when they took their letters to catch the midnight post. They would see each other home, stopping on each other's doorsteps, unwilling to end their fascinating talk which would often go on into the small hours.' Pepler was an advocate for social improvement and wrote a radical pamphlet promoting a more natural approach to the upbringing of babies. In his capacity as a social worker with the London County Council he introduced the first school meals into the capital's schools.

Pepler and his family moved to Ditchling in 1913, taking over the Gills' old home, Sopers. At this time Gill, Johnston and Pepler spent huge amounts of time together, tramping the downs, talking late into the night and producing together an eclectic little magazine, *The Game*. In 1916 Pepler founded St Dominic's Press and the following year converted to Catholicism (he had been brought up a Quaker). From Sopers Pepler again followed his friend Gill in 1918, this time moving his large family of six children, and the press, into a newly built house on a farm called Halletts, on the edge of Ditchling Common. He later bought Fragbarrow Farm on the Common, which he ran with his son David. In 1920 he co-founded with Gill, Desmond Chute and Joseph Cribb the Guild of SS Joseph & Dominic.

Pepler was always more integrated with the village than Gill and by 1923 serious tensions had developed between the two men. Pepler wanted to extend the scope of the Catholic community and even took up the office of Reeve of Ditchling Common. Each had differing views on how the finances of the Guild should be organised (Gill referred to Pepler as 'Hilario Bottomlessfinance'). The engagement of Pepler's son David to Gill's eldest daughter, Betty, did nothing to ease the situation (they later married). After Gill left Ditchling Common, Pepler again moved into his friend's old home – this time it was Hopkins Crank – and remained there until his death. He developed a keen interest in puppeteering and mime, working for the BBC and even touring the United States lecturing and performing mime. St Dominic's Press came to a sad end after Pepler was expelled from the Guild in 1934. He refused to back down after the press had employed a non-Catholic assistant and sought to mechanise one of the presses. The press continued to publish until 1937, by which time his son Mark had relaunched it as the Ditchling Press with premises in the village High Street (located where silversmiths Pruden and Smith now work).

Dunstan Pruden 1907-74 *Silversmith*

Originally known as Alfred Charles, Pruden changed his name to Dunstan when he converted to Roman Catholicism. He arrived in Ditchling in 1932 and became a full member of the Guild of SS Joseph & Dominic two years later. He gained international recognition as a maker of ecclesiastical gold and silver work. He wrote *Silversmithing*, published by St Dominic's Press, and also taught at Brighton College of Art, becoming Head of Silversmithing there. His second wife, Winefride, was also a silversmith and Guild member.

John Skelton MBE 1923-99 *Sculptor & Lettercutter*

A nephew of Eric Gill (his mother, Angela, was Gill's youngest sister), Skelton became apprentice to Gill at Piggots for the last few months of the artist's life. He moved to Ditchling Common after Gill's death to train with Joseph Cribb. Following active service in WWII and study at Coventry School of Art, he returned to Ditchling and married the silversmith Myrtle Bromley Martin. They set up a workshop at Burgess Hill, which they moved to the small village of Streat in 1958. Skelton worked in several other mediums apart from stone, including metal and silver; he also drew and painted in watercolour. His daughter Helen Mary Skelton worked with him and now runs the workshop in Streat.

DITCHLING VILLAGE
INFORMATION

The lovely village of Ditchling lies within the South Downs National Park and has easy access to the much larger and bustling towns of Burgess Hill, Haywards Heath, Lewes and the coastal city of Brighton. Located near the border between East and West Sussex, it is the perfect rural setting for exploring the large county of Sussex. Ordnance Survey map 122 is a useful guide to seeing the area on foot.

Transport

If travelling by car, parking in the centre of the village is available behind the village hall in Lewes Road. There are also car parks at Ditchling Beacon and Ditchling Common Country Park. Ditchling is about three miles from the M23/A23 Pyecombe and Hassocks junction.

The nearest train station is Hassocks, just over a mile away (visit *www.nationalrail.co.uk* for details). There are several local, if infrequent, bus services, contact *www.travellinesoutheast.org.uk* or call 0871 200 2233 for details. Compass Travel operate some bus routes that include Ditchling, visit *www.compass-travel.co.uk* or call 01903 690020 for more information. During the summer months a bus service runs from Brighton and Hove, called Breeze Up The Downs; you can find out more about it at *www.brighton-hove.gov.uk* or call 01273 290000.

Accommodation

Some Bed and Breakfast accommodation is available locally, visit *www.sussex-southdowns-guide.com* for up-to-date information. There are several camping sites in the area including Ditchling Camping (visit *www.ditchlingcamp.co.uk* or call 07733 103309), Blackberry Wood (visit *www.blackberrywood.com* or call 01273 890035), Stoneywish Camping (visit *www.stoneywish.co.uk* or call 01273 843498) and Southdown Way

Caravan and Camping Park (visit *www.southdown-cararvancamping.org.uk* or call 01273 841877). Both of Ditchling's public houses offer accommodation; The White Horse is located in West Street (visit *www.whitehorseditchling.com* or call 01273 842006) and The Bull is in the High Street and can be contacted on 01273 843147 (visit *www.thebullditchling.com*).

Some useful contact details

DITCHLING BEACON, NATIONAL TRUST *www.nationaltrust.org.uk*

DITCHLING COMMON COUNTRY PARK visit *www.eastsussex.gov.uk* or call 01273 482670.

DITCHLING HISTORY PROJECT visit
www.ditchlinghistoryproject.org

DITCHLING MUSEUM OF ART + CRAFT visit
www.ditchlingmuseumartcraft.org.uk or call 01273 844744.

THE DITCHLING SOCIETY *www.ditchlingsociety.wordpress.com*

SOUTH DOWNS NATIONAL PARK visit *www.southdowns.gov.uk* or call 01730 814810.

VISIT DITCHLING *www.visitditchling.co.uk*

SUGGESTED READING

Keith Alldritt
David Jones Writer & Artist
Constable, 2003

Mike Burr & Tom Dufty
Ditchling in Detail
2008

Edgar Holloway
Capel-y-ffin to Ditchling, Watercolour Drawings by Edgar Holloway
Ditchling Museum, 2000

Ewan Clayton
Edward Johnston: Lettering & Life
Ditchling Museum, 2007

Margot Coatts
A Weaver's Life Ethel Mairet 1872-1952
Crafts Council, 1983

Janet & David Cragg
Exploring Ditchling, Ten Circular Walks
SB Publications, 1995

Ruth Cribb & Joe Cribb
Eric Gill & Ditchling: the Workshop Tradition
Ditchling Museum, 2007

Ruth Cribb & Joe Cribb
Eric Gill
British Museum Press, 2011

Susan Falkner
A Ditchling Childhood 1916-1936
Iceni Publications, 1994

Eric Gill
Autobiography
Jonathan Cape, 1940

Lottie Hoare
Philip Hagreen: A Sceptic & A Craftsman
Ritchie Press, 2009

Charles Knight
Landscapes by Charles Knight 1901-1990
Chris Beetles Limited, 1997

Fiona MacCarthy
Eric Gill
Faber and Faber, 1989

Diana de Vere Cole
Brangwyn in Perspective
The One Root Press, 2006

Walk Around Ditchling Village
Ditchling History Project
2007

ACKNOWLEDGEMENTS

S pecial thanks to my long-standing friends Raymond Briggs and John Vernon Lord for their help and advice and to Raymond for sharing his very amusing memories of his early encounters with the village of Ditchling.

Many thanks to Jenny KilBride and Joe Cribb for their careful reading of my text and their very helpful suggestions. Thanks too to Adam Ford for his time and helpful comments. Also to Nathaniel Hepburn, Geraldine Warner and the staff at Ditchling Museum of Art + Craft.

Thanks to Helen Mary Skelton for providing information about her family and for help with the walk to Streat.

Thanks also to Janet Hale and the staff at St George's Retreat.

Many thanks to Sarah Young for providing such lovely maps and for being, as always, a pleasure to work with.

Picture credits

COVER IMAGE *Ditchling Village* by Eric Gill.

Pages 16, 28, 50, 56 and 60 wood engravings by Eric Gill taken from *Woodwork* (In Principle and Practice) Vol.1 by A. Romney Green, printed and published by Douglas Pepler, Ditchling, 1918.

Page 44 wood engraving by Eric Gill from *The Game* Vol.IV September 1921.

INDEX

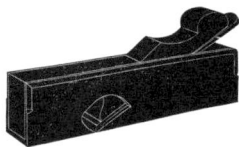